# MEGGAN WILSON

# A CREATIVE REBEL'S GUIDE TO WINNING THE GAME OF LIFE

# JACOB WILSON

Copyright © 2022 by The Creative Rebel Company LLC

ISBN: 978-1-956910-01-8

Cover design: Murphy Rae, www.murphyrae.com

All rights reserved. No part of this book may be reproduced or transmitted in any form or by any means, electronic or mechanical, including photocopying, recording, or by any information storage and retrieval system without the prior written permission of The Creative Rebel Company LLC.

The authors and publisher of this book do not dispense professional or medical advice or prescribe the use of any technique for the diagnosis or treatment of any physical, mental, emotional, or medical condition. The intent of the authors is to offer information as part of the reader's health, wellness, and spiritual journey. The reader should consult his or her own medical or other trusted health professional before implementing any suggestions contained in this book, and if any such suggestions are implemented, then the authors and publisher assume no responsibility for the direct or indirect consequences.

                    Visit our website at www.creativerebel.com

# A CREATIVE REBEL'S GUIDE TO WINNING THE GAME OF LIFE

**Meggan Wilson and Jacob Wilson**

The Creative Rebel Company

# CONTENTS

| | |
|---|---|
| About *A Creative Rebel's Guide to Winning the Game of Life* | vii |
| Introduction | xi |
| Chapter 1<br>*Your Magical Self* | 1 |
| Chapter 2<br>*Secrets of the Universe* | 9 |
| Chapter 3<br>*Consciousness: The Final Frontier* | 19 |
| Chapter 4<br>*Words are Powerful* | 35 |
| Chapter 5<br>*Writing Your Own Story* | 41 |
| Chapter 6<br>*Falling in Love with You* | 47 |
| Chapter 7<br>*Karma, the Divine Plan, and the Safety Switch on your Power* | 61 |
| Chapter 8<br>*Helping Your Dreams Come True* | 69 |
| Chapter 9<br>*Change Your Habits, Change Your Life* | 83 |
| Chapter 10<br>*Health is Wealth* | 107 |
| Chapter 11<br>*Wealth, Success, and Living Well* | 141 |
| A Final Word | 167 |
| Bonus | 169 |
| Who Are We? | 171 |
| Acknowledgments | 175 |
| Notes | 177 |

# ABOUT *A CREATIVE REBEL'S GUIDE TO WINNING THE GAME OF LIFE*

**What do you do when you feel like you've won the game of life?**
*Share the secrets you've learned so everyone else can win too!*

At least, that's what we decided to do.

After all, we didn't set out to win *anything* when we each took a chance on ourselves and followed our hearts. We both just knew there had to be something more than the unfulfilling lives we were living. We each took a step and the Universe rose up to meet us—taking us on a wild adventure up the mountain of success, health, fitness, happiness, love, fulfillment, and inner peace.

Now, we wake up every day feeling like we've won the game of life. How could we possibly keep all this goodness to ourselves?

*A Creative Rebel's Guide to Winning the Game of Life* is brought to you by the minds behind the blockbuster *New York Times,* #1 *Wall Street Journal*, and *USA Today* bestselling romance brand Meghan March—the epic wife and husband team, Meggan and Jacob Wilson.

Prepare yourself for self-help like you've never read before. Books are magic. They can change your life—especially this one.

*To the Light,
with Love.*

# INTRODUCTION

I don't know if anyone has told you this lately, but you're amazing. Truly, incredibly, without a single doubt—*amazing*.

Not just because you're a miracle for even being born, which you are, but because you are so *freaking* powerful and you may not even know it yet.

If you're thinking—are you really talking about me? Yes. With 100 percent certainty, I am talking about *you*.

Somewhere along the lines of history, the true nature of what and who we really are became obscured. Throughout the ages, people have hunted for the truth, and over and over again, they have landed on the same conclusion:

**WE ARE EACH THE ALL-POWERFUL MASTER OF OUR OWN UNIVERSE, IF WE BUT KNEW AND UNDERSTOOD THE POWER AND AUTHORITY WE HAVE BEEN GIFTED.**

This includes you.

*You* are magical. You have wonderful powers that can create for you the life of your dreams. We know. Because we've done it. We've walked this road, and it led us to the most wonderful, incredible discoveries and a life so amazing that we didn't even know it was possible to live it. But it is.

And before you think, *just because they did it doesn't mean I can*, hang with us.

I was an overweight, overstressed, overmedicated, in-debt-up-to-my-eyeballs, sick, and depressed lost soul living paycheck to paycheck who hated her job and wanted a different life.

Jake was a partier, constantly getting into fights, broke on the regular, occasionally selling drugs to get by, and working dead-end and odd jobs that were taking him nowhere.

At different times and in different ways—and completely separately—we woke up to the fact that if we wanted to change our lives and ourselves, it was up to us. We each took a risk. We decided to do something for ourselves, for our lives. To do something beyond what we'd been taught to do. We took control of our lives and put our power to work for us—even if we didn't exactly know what we were doing at the time. What happened next was beyond our wildest dreams.

We changed. Radically.

Our lives changed. Radically.

Our paths then brought us together in the most magical, incredible way imaginable, so life could take us on an even more amazing journey. A journey that led us here. To you.

Now we can tell you what happens when you take a step in the right direction and do something constructive for yourself.

### YOU CHANGE EVERYTHING.

Now, we're both happy, healthy, wealthy, and peaceful vibrant souls living the life of our dreams together. We wake up every day thanking God for the magic that is our life.

Transformations like this aren't unique to us.

*Anyone can do it*. And that includes *you*.

If you resonate with wanting a different life or to transform yourself into a happy, free, love-filled being living the life of your dreams, then you've been led to this book intentionally, by the very genius of the Universe.

Ten years ago, neither of us knew a transformation like this was possible for us. We thought incredible lives only happened to other people or "special" people. Neither of us had any idea that this could be true for us too. We didn't know it could be true for everyone. *But it is.*

Anyone can live a healthy, wealthy, happy, truly abundant, joyful, peace- and love-filled existence. So, why isn't everyone living like that already?

### BECAUSE IT DOESN'T JUST HAPPEN *TO* YOU. IT HAPPENS *THROUGH* YOU.

If you want to change your life, all you have to do is work on yourself. *Change yourself.* That's it. There's truly nothing else for you to change. *Ever.*

You are the key to everything. *You* are magic, and you have the power to transform yourself and your life. You have this power at every moment. It's free to use and you can do it right where you are, with exactly what you have, and you don't need anyone else's permission to do it.

Doesn't that sound awesome? It is.

But if it still sounds hard for you to believe right now, it's only because you've been conditioned and programmed to believe otherwise. That's okay. This is something you can learn. *Anyone can.* If you want to transform yourself and your life, it's the most necessary thing you will ever learn.

Here's the bottom line:

### WE ARE ALL ACTUALLY INCREDIBLY POWERFUL BEINGS WHO CREATE OUR OWN REALITIES AND HAVE EVERYTHING INSIDE US THAT IT TAKES TO MAKE OUR DREAMS COME TRUE.

*You* are the ruler of your universe. *You* are the king of your world. *You* decide who you're going to be. *You* decide what kind of future you are going to have.

We have proven this over and over in our own lives and have watched as others have proven it too. This isn't conjecture. This is the truth, and it's time to shine a brighter light on it so you can become the hero of your own story, even if you don't think you are right now.

The purpose of this book is to help you understand who and what you really are, how this life of ours really works, where your power lies, how to use it wisely, and ways to become the person you've always wanted to be and create the life of your dreams.

However, like most of the best things in life, this is a do-it-yourself project. No one else can do this for you. You can't even pay someone to do it for you.

**YOU HAVE TO CHOOSE TO DO IT FOR YOURSELF, AND ACTUALLY *DO IT FOR YOURSELF*.**

It takes work. It takes effort. But that's all part of the journey. Thankfully, the rewards are exponentially greater than any effort you will expend.

Open your mind or prepare to have it blown repeatedly. Drop your judgments and preconceived notions at the door. Prepare to see things differently. Prepare to see *yourself* differently. Because you are magical and possess power far beyond anything you may have ever realized could be possible.

Like with all books of this nature, take what resonates with you and leave the rest. Then try it. Apply it. Prove it for yourself.

No one else gets to decide your future for you—unless you let them. It's time to take your power back and start becoming the person you were meant to be so you can get on with living the life you came here to live.

# ONE
## YOUR MAGICAL SELF

> You must first have the knowledge of your power; second, the courage to dare; and third, the faith to do.
> – Charles F. Haanel

**Who are you exactly?**

What's the first thing that popped into your head when you read that question? Was it your name? Your occupation? Your familial status? A label you wear? Or something else?

Jake and I would have described ourselves in that way before too. That was, until we learned some things we'd never been taught.

First, let's get a few basics down:

You are not your body. You have a body.
You are not your occupation. You have an occupation.
You are not your labels. You choose to have labels.
You are not your thoughts. You have thoughts.
You are not your ego. You have an ego.
You are not your mind. You have access to your mind.
You are not your emotions. You have emotions.

If you're not any of these things, then what are you?

You are so much more than what you see when you look in a mirror. You are a multidimensional being of pure energy and light that has incarnated on Earth in this lifetime in order to play an active role in the unfolding of the Divine Plan orchestrated by the Infinite Intelligence of the Universe itself.

You are eternal. You are infinite. You have latent inside you all of the powers that exist in the Universe. You are so powerful that no one truly knows what you're capable of.

When we say you're magical, we're not just spouting hyperbole. You really are.

## Wait, I'm really magical?

You may find it hard to believe that you're magical, but even you—oh, doubting one—might feel a little glimmer of something inside you that wants that statement to be true. Maybe you're afraid we're full of crap, but you *want to believe it*. That's a sign you should keep reading.

We've been led to believe for most of our lives that we are simply human bodies, living only this single life, and that all of our thoughts come from the brains in our skulls, and we have little control over what happens to us. We've been led to believe that only special people get to be healthy, fit, happy, wealthy, successful, find fulfillment, find true love, or live awesome lives. We've been led to believe that bad things just happen, without any reason or discernable cause.

This is all patently untrue.

We've been led to believe wrongly. But that's fine, because all that matters, if this information is new to you, is that you're finding out the truth *now* so you can do something with it.

What can you do with this knowledge?

Anything. The possibilities are truly limitless.

## Back to the Beginning

You are a free-will being living in an energetic universe. *Everything* is energy. What does that mean? Well, if you want to know the truth, we're going to have to go somewhere you probably didn't expect—back to the Source of everything.

It doesn't matter what you call Source—the Universe, Infinite Intelligence, God, Source Energy, Spirit, Holy Spirit, Great Spirit, Goddess, Divine Mother, Brahma, Allah, Father, the Creator, the Divine, the Infinite, the Presence, the Field, the Aether, etc. The name doesn't matter. Don't get hung up on that.

Society has all sorts of programming back through the ages to make you feel certain ways about certain words. Don't let it trigger you, or you'll be forfeiting so much knowledge that's out there and available to you—if you can just drop your baggage about certain words. Because truly, the word you use to describe Source does not matter. We will use all sorts of different words, because we refer to It in all sorts of different ways in our daily life.

What matters is that you know that Source Energy is real, powerful, and constantly at work in your life, in your body, and all around you. In fact, It is what we are made from. It is what *everything that exists or will ever exist* is made from.

Plato and Aristotle called it the First Cause. It is the visible and the invisible. The manifest and the unmanifest. It is All That Is. Without Source, nothing would be here . . . except for It. By itself. Alone. Just like It was in the beginning.

Yogananda, an enlightened Indian mystic, put it beautifully:

> [W]hen the ocean of space was unpeopled, uninhabited by floating island universes, when the sun and moon and planetary families did not swim in space, when the little ball of earth with its dollhouses and diminutive human beings did not exist, when no object of any kind had come into being—Spirit existed.[1]

Spirit was here first. Spirit will be here last. That's because *everything* is Spirit.

In the 2002 film adaptation of *The Count of Monte Cristo*, the screenwriter speaks through Alexandre Dumas' character Mercedes when she says about God, "He is in everything."[2] The truth is often buried in fiction. I know, because as an author, I did it all the time.

God is everywhere. God is in everything. In fact—open your mind here—*you* are a manifestation of God, experiencing life as your individual personality.

We know that might sound complicated and be a lot to swallow, especially so early in this book. But unlike with fiction novels, there's no point in dragging you through hundreds of pages before the shocking twist is revealed.

If you think about it, this all actually makes sense. After all, if you were a limitless, unending, all-powerful, brilliant energy of infinite intelligence, pure unconditional love and full of joy, would you want to be alone forever? Or would you want someone to share your love and joy and experiences with?

When Jake and I went on our first date, he said something to me that shifted my very being—something pretty common with him, I learned. I was telling him about how I wanted to travel all over the world and see everything and experience it all. His question to me was, "How much fun will that be if you have no one to share it with?"

The realization hit me hard. I didn't want to experience all that magic by myself. I wanted someone to enjoy it with me.

Well, Spirit didn't want to spend infinity and eternity alone either. Hence, the vastness of our universe and everything in it—including you. In fact, *individual* originally meant *indivisible*, as in, cannot be separated from the whole.

According to the first edition of *Webster's New International Dictionary*, these are considered "obsolete" meanings of *individual*:

> *1. Not divisible;* of *one essence or nature; indiscerptible, and*

*2. Not to be parted; inseparable.*[3]

If you take a step back and look at the big picture, you can see why this is such a big deal.

## WE ARE ALL *ONE*.
## WE ARE ALL INSEPARABLE PARTS OF SOURCE.
## WE ARE ALL MADE *OUT OF SOURCE*, BECAUSE SOURCE IS LITERALLY ALL THAT IS.

That's a big realization to make.

It also seems like an important concept to leave out of most of our formative educations. Or maybe it was left out by design, so each of us could find our own way back to the truth. Back to the knowledge of who and what we really are.

This might not have been where you expected this book to be going, but when we sat down to write the truth, we couldn't leave it out. It's too important. It's the linchpin that makes everything about us and our magic make sense.

Because if you search long enough for answers, you're going to end up back at the beginning. Back at the Source of *everything*.

Which is actually awesome.

When you realize you're made out of Infinite Intelligence, you realize you are endowed with limitless powers, abilities, possibilities, and potential. You literally are *magic*.

You create your own reality—with Infinite Intelligence. That's why it is called co-creating. Everything that God is and has is available to *you*. What's more, it's all innate within *you*.

But here's another thing you need to know:

## WHILE GOD IS ALL THAT YOU ARE, GOD IS ALSO *SO MUCH MORE THAN WHAT YOU ARE*.

Source is all-knowing, all-seeing, and all-powerful. Or if you prefer, omniscient, omnipresent, and omnipotent.

Source is the single power responsible for everything in the Universe. Source keeps the planets moving in precise paths that can be calculated hundreds of years into the future. Source keeps the sun rising and setting. Source keeps you and every other person on Earth breathing and our hearts beating and our nerves and synapses firing. The reality of Source is so vast that it is unknowable and incomprehensible in its entirety.

Sages and gurus throughout the ages have acknowledged that you can never know all of God. But you can know yourself.

It was inscribed at the temple of Apollo at Delphi in Greece:

**Know Thyself**

When you know yourself, it's the closest you may ever get to understanding Infinite Intelligence, even if you don't exactly resonate with the idea of *being* Infinite Intelligence yet. That's okay. You'll get there. This is a journey. A journey that's a big part of the reason you incarnated. To find your way back home. To who you truly are. To find your way back to your magic.

Because *you are magic.* There's probably a small part of you—or maybe a big piece—that wants to believe this is all true. Because, wouldn't it be just the coolest thing ever to have the power to change your life at any given moment and put yourself on a course to living with joy and abundance every day? It is awesome because you do have that power, and it's time to start learning about it so you can use it and fulfill your Divine destiny.

Thankfully, there's a shift in the works. The human collective is moving from a fear-based existence to a love- and heart-centered existence, even if it doesn't exactly seem like it. It is happening. It's been prophesied for thousands of years. A new Golden Age is coming into manifestation on Earth, where all beings will be happy and free. When exactly that's going to happen, no one knows. But Divine Timing is absolutely perfect.

In the meantime, you don't have to wait for a global shift to come about to become the person you've always wanted to be and to live an incredible, abundant life that fills you with joy, happiness, fulfillment, and love.

You can start working on that right now.

# TWO
## SECRETS OF THE UNIVERSE

> If you want to know the secrets of the universe, think in terms of energy, frequency, and vibration.
> – Nikola Tesla

Everything is energy—including you. And because everything is energy, everything has a vibration and a frequency at every given moment. Everything you see around you that appears to be solid is actually a bunch of vibrating particles. They appear solid because they're vibrating slowly.

Remember when you were taught the difference between solids, liquids, and gasses? They can all be the same particle, but they are vibrating at different speeds. For instance, $H_2O$ can appear as ice, water, or steam.

Other things vibrate at much greater speeds, so fast that you can't see them. These include your thoughts, your words, and your emotions. They are all energy too.

If you've ever thought that you didn't matter or that your life, thoughts, words, emotions, beliefs, and decisions weren't really that important in the grand scheme of things, we have ground-breaking news for you: you thought wrong.

This life that you're living is *all about you* and what you're doing with it. After all, the energy flowing through you right now is a gift from Source. You're using Source's power in every breath you take, word you speak, thought you think, emotion you feel, and action you take.

You matter. You matter *so much*. Your thoughts matter. Your words matter. How you feel matters. What you believe matters. What you do matters.

Why?

Because every single thought you think, word you say, belief you hold, and emotion you feel has a vibration and a frequency. Vibrations and frequencies *do not lie*. They are what they are.

As you can probably imagine, different types of thoughts, words, feelings, and beliefs have different vibrations and frequencies. This becomes really important because it's the basis of a Universal Law that you might have heard about before: the Law of Attraction.

The Law of Attraction isn't just about manifesting a new job, a raise, or a great partner. It's actually the basis of how you create your entire reality. And if you've never heard of the Law of Attraction before, don't worry. It's really simple:

**LIKE ATTRACTS LIKE.**

You've probably heard the phrases *birds of a feather flock together* or *misery loves company*. These are examples of the Law of Attraction in action.

But what does it mean on a practical level for you and your life?

Your life is a reflection of what you think about consistently and emotionalize. Ralph Waldo Emerson nailed it when he said, "You become what you think about all day long."

However, before we delve into your thoughts themselves, we need to make a quick pit stop to learn about how your mind works, because knowledge is power, and it's time to take yours back.

## Your Mind

In *The Power of Your Subconscious Mind*, Dr. Joseph Murphy explains:

> You have a mind, and you should learn how to use it. There are two levels of your mind—the conscious or rational level, and the subconscious or irrational level. You think with your conscious mind, and whatever you habitually think about sinks down into your subconscious mind, which creates according to the nature of your thoughts. Your subconscious mind is the seat of your emotions and is the creative mind. If you think good, good will follow; if you think evil, evil will follow. This is the way the mind works.[1]

Dr. Murphy is right—you should learn how to use your mind. Your mind is incredible. Your subconscious mind is your connection to the Infinite—to *everything*. And if you don't know how to use it properly, there's a high likelihood that someone else who does know is using it for you to create the reality that *they want*.

No joke. This is for real. Tons of people know how this stuff works, and many will not hesitate to exploit your ignorance and use it in ways that are not favorable to you. You have every incentive in the world to get your mind to work *for you* rather than against you.

Maybe Dr. Murphy wasn't calling you magical, but you are. Your mind, under your conscious control, is absolutely limitless. What you do with it matters. The thoughts you think are powerful. They dictate the course and quality of your life.

Dr. Murphy adds:

> Your subconscious mind accepts what is impressed upon it or what you consciously believe. It does not reason things out like your conscious mind, and it does not argue with you controversially.

Your subconscious mind is like the soil, which accepts any kind of seed, good or bad.[2]

Only you get to decide the seeds you're planting. Choose carefully, because as Dr. Murphy explains, "once the subconscious mind accepts an idea, it begins to execute it."[3]

To break it down:

**Whatever you believe to be true or accept to be true or assume to be true—your subconscious mind goes to work *making it true in your reality*. It doesn't matter what that belief is.**

Dr. David R. Hawkins, in *Truth vs. Falsehood: How to Tell the Difference*, takes us another step further and gives us more powerful knowledge:

The design of the human mind is also comparable to that of a computer in which the brain is the hardware that is capable of playing any software programs fed into it. The hardware is, by design, incapable of protecting itself from false information; therefore, the mind will believe any software program with which society has programmed it, for it is innocently without any safeguard or protection.[4]

Think about what Dr. Murphy and Dr. Hawkins are saying. Not only is your mind wildly powerful and your thoughts and beliefs wildly important, but everything you believe has been programmed into you like you're a computer. At the time it was programmed into you, your brain couldn't tell the difference between what was true and what was false. That means there's a good possibility that you currently believe things that are not true. Things that are not leading you to the life of your dreams or helping you become the person you were meant to be when you incarnated in this body.

This is especially true about things that you were told, shown, or that were modeled to you between birth and age six.[5] During that time period, kids are veritable sponges because they're in the delta and theta brain wave states, believing everything they're told as absolute fact, as it downloads directly into their subconscious.[6] It's not by accident, though—it's by design. Part of the journey that you're taking through this life is figuring out all the untrue beliefs you've been programmed with, so that you can change the programs and change your life.

What's more, 95 percent of your subconscious beliefs are running in the background, below the level of your awareness.[7] They are an invisible force shaping your life and who you're becoming at every moment. Don't worry though, you can change them. You can *always change everything*.

## YOU ARE IN CONTROL HERE. NO ONE ELSE.

The first step is becoming aware of how much power you have so you can start paying attention to how you're using it.

### Thoughts Are Powerful

Your thoughts are not invisible things that no one else can ever find out about because they're simply in your head and don't matter. That's not true at all. Your thoughts are actually energetic packets of information that are being impressed into your subconscious and the very fabric of the Universe.

The degree and intensity to which you emotionalize a thought and how often you think it determines what it creates in your life. To put it another way: if you feel really strongly about something and you think about it all the time, you're increasing the likelihood that that thought or some form of it will manifest in your life—good or bad. Thoughts become things.

Let's pause, because this is really important to understand.

## YOUR THOUGHTS BECOME THINGS.

This is the process of creation. It all starts in your mind with a thought. The thoughts you think are the reason you are who you are right now, and they are responsible for the life you're currently living.

If you don't currently love your life, you might be thinking: *Wait, you're saying I'm responsible for the current state of my life and everything in it?*

Yes. You are.

It's not always the most enjoyable realization when it first hits you, but it can definitely be one of the most powerful. This is the moment you realize that *you* are in control. There are no inexplicable forces out there acting on you maliciously or deliberately, trying to make life difficult for you. We manage to do that quite effectively all by ourselves.

If you've ever thought you were your own worst enemy, you were right. But that's okay. You've been playing this game of life where no one told you the rules. So far, you've had to figure this all out by trial and error, relying on guidance that sounded good at the time, or at least was the best you could find. Plus, your brain couldn't tell if what you were learning was true or false. You've been playing with a handicap, just like almost everyone else on the planet. You're doing just fine. Everything's okay. Don't worry.

The Universe led you to this book because you're in the right place, right *now* to do something about it. Because this is the beautiful thing: if doing what you did got you to where you are, then doing something different is going to take you somewhere else. All you have to do is give it a shot and have some faith in yourself. After all, you're powerful beyond measure.

## CHANGE YOUR THOUGHTS, AND YOU WILL CHANGE YOUR LIFE.

## The Law of Attraction

Esther and Jerry Hicks, with their guide, Abraham, wrote the book *The Law of Attraction,* and in it they share many details on the practical workings of this law. One of the most important things to realize is this: "You get the essence of what you are thinking about, whether it is something you want or something you do not want."[8]

This aligns with what Dr. Murphy stated as well. Why? Because your thoughts are *magnetic*. As Abraham explains:

> The *Law of Attraction* and its magnetic power reaches out into the Universe and attracts other thoughts that are vibrationally like it . . . and brings that to you: Your attention to subjects, your activation of thoughts, and the *Law of Attraction*'s response to those thoughts is responsible for every person, every event, and every circumstance that comes into your experience.[9]

Your thoughts are the starting point for creating your life. The Law of Attraction takes it from there, bringing you more similar thoughts, as well as people and experiences who match the vibration of your thoughts.

This is why when you're in a crap mood, you're more likely to have a crap day. Or if something goes wrong in the morning and you focus your attention on it and think about it, *even more* stuff starts going wrong. It's not an accident. You brought it into your experience with your mind, in conjunction with the workings of Universal Law. That's how this works.

Dr. Joe Dispenza explains it fabulously in *Becoming Supernatural:*

> When we think a thought, those networks of neurons that fire in our brain create electrical charges. When those thoughts also cause a chemical reaction that results in a feeling or an emotion . . . those feelings create *magnetic* changes. They merge with the thoughts

that create the electric charges to produce a specific electromagnetic field equal to your state of being. Think of emotions as *energy in motion*.[10]

The thoughts you think and the emotions you feel are literally creating an electromagnetic field all around your body. All electromagnetic fields have a frequency. And just like a radio where you only get what's playing on the station you're tuned into, *you only attract things on the same frequency that your personal electromagnetic field is emitting.*

That's why your crap mood leads to a crap day. This is why what you feel matters so much. When you're angry, you attract more people, experiences, and events into your life to give you more reasons to feel angry. When you're grateful, you attract more people, experiences, and events into your life to give you more reasons to feel grateful. Same with hate, judgment, fear, love, excitement, joy, etc. It doesn't matter what the emotion is; it's combining with your thoughts to dictate the course of your life.

And while it seems obvious that most people would prefer to be living a life where experiences are always evoking love, joy, excitement, and gratitude, rather than hate, judgment, anger, and fear, there's also an important reason why sometimes it's hard to make the jump.

You're not only an electromagnetic being, you're also an electrochemical being. As Dr. Joe Dispenza described above, your thoughts create chemical reactions in your body. If you're constantly thinking the same kinds of thoughts, your body constantly produces the same kinds of chemical cocktails. This is where it gets shocking.

> "[O]ur bodies become so conditioned to this rush of chemicals that they become addicted to them. Our bodies actually crave them."[11]

That's right. Your body can become *addicted* to emotions.

Have you ever felt *good* when you were angry? If you have, your body may have been jonesing for a fix of that particular chemical cocktail and perhaps is addicted to it.

What's more, because you're broadcasting it in your electromagnetic field, your world is serving up more reasons for you to get angry so you can feed that addiction.

But you can absolutely break the cycle. You can overcome the addiction your body may have to certain emotions that aren't serving your future. The first step is awareness. Knowledge is power.

If you don't like what you're currently experiencing, only you have the power to change it. You're the only one who can change your thoughts and emotions—and the course of your life.

The power has always been in your hands.

# THREE
## CONSCIOUSNESS: THE FINAL FRONTIER

*Great things are done by people who think great thoughts and then go out into the world to make their dreams come true.*
– Ernest Holmes

The most important thoughts you ever think are those you think about yourself.

Your self-concept—the story you tell yourself about yourself in your head—is the most important story of your entire life. Who you think you are, you are—or you are in the process of becoming. When you change the story about who you are in your mind, you change your life. Why? Because you take the first step to changing who you are being.

You take the first step to changing your *consciousness*.

### Consciousness is Everything

Your consciousness is expressed by who you are being. You demonstrate your current state of consciousness with every thought, word, decision, emotion, action, and reaction.

If you are poor, you are expressing poverty consciousness. If you are rich, you are expressing wealth consciousness. If you are sick, you are expressing illness consciousness. If you are healthy, you are expressing a consciousness of health. The same can be said of every other state of being you could possibly find yourself in.

## YOUR CONSCIOUSNESS IS EXPRESSED BY WHO YOU ARE BEING.

If you are being tight-fisted with money and begrudge giving it to others because you are worried you will not have enough for yourself, you are expressing a consciousness of scarcity and lack. If you share and give generously, never worrying about where your supply will come from or whether it will run out, you are expressing a consciousness of lavish abundance.

Your expression of consciousness comes from what you believe about *yourself* and *the world*.

Consciousness is the ultimate adventure in life. The final frontier. The giver of all gifts. It is the fullness of the Godhead, and the magic endowed to us by our Creator. If you love your life, it's because of your consciousness. If you don't, it's also because of your consciousness.

The best part about understanding consciousness is this:

## YOU CAN CHANGE YOUR CONSCIOUSNESS AND CHANGE YOUR LIFE.

It's time to take a look in the mirror—literally and figuratively—to start figuring out who you are being.

Not *who you are. Who you are being.*

If I asked you to tell me who you are, you wouldn't necessarily be as honest about it. That's okay. It's human nature. Who likes to get super honest about all of their flaws and failings and truly take stock of how they're really doing in life? Not everyone. It's our shadows that we're afraid of in the dark. Not our light.

But it doesn't matter whether it's fun, sometimes you have to take stock of your life and get radically honest with yourself.

Remember the Greek temple—know thyself?

This is the point at which change can happen.

Here's the truth:

**THE ONLY THING YOU CAN TRULY CHANGE IN THIS LIFE, WITH LASTING IMPACT, IS YOURSELF.**

But that's all you truly need the power to change.

Why?

When you change yourself, you change your consciousness, and then everything else in your life that does not match your new self-concept and your new consciousness *has to change*. It's law. When you change yourself, the things around you have to change.

This is how radical transformation, like Jake and I have both experienced, takes place. We changed who we were being, and the laws of the Universe did the rest.

Up until this point in your life, you might have spent a lot of time and energy trying to change the things outside of you.

For example, when some people aren't happy in relationships, they tend to break up and go looking for someone "better." Then after the honeymoon phase wears off with the "better" partner, they're not sure why they're not happy in the new relationship either.

Why does that happen?

It's actually an easy answer.

**YOU TAKE YOURSELF WITH YOU WHEREVER YOU GO. YOU TAKE YOUR CONSCIOUSNESS WITH YOU WHEREVER YOU GO.**

It's only by changing the *cause* that you can make real and lasting changes in the *effects*. Trying to change anything *outside* of you without first changing something *inside* of you is trying to change the effects without changing the cause. As you may have experienced, it's hard and doesn't always stick. This is why jumping from partner to partner without changing *yourself* first usually results in the same outcome of an unfulfilling relationship.

If you want a different outcome, *you* have to change. And to change, you have to change your consciousness.

"It is only by a change of consciousness, by actually changing your concept of yourself that you can 'build more stately mansions'—the manifestations of higher and higher concepts," says Neville Goddard in *The Power of Awareness*.[1] He adds, "[C]onsciousness is the one and only reality, it is the first and only cause-substance of the phenomena of life."[2]

Everything in your entire life is an out-picturing of your current state of consciousness. *Everything*. This is the perfection of Source. What you believe yourself to be—*you are*—or you are in the process of becoming.

The only time your current state of consciousness is not out-pictured perfectly in your life is at the moment you change it and the moments after, during which the outer world is catching up with the new inner you. In order for those changes in your outer world to manifest, you have to sustain your new consciousness long enough for the material world of effect to catch up with the invisible world of cause. And it will, as long as you persist in continuing to be the new you—regardless of what things look like around you.

This is why the concept of "fake it until you make it" works. Because you are persisting in your new state of consciousness despite all appearances to the contrary.

Another important point: you don't see and experience the world as it truly is. You see and experience the world as you *believe it to be*. You control your beliefs. You are in control of what you see and experience through your consciousness.

This is how it works in a nutshell:

**SOURCE ENERGY POURS THROUGH YOU AS UNADULTERATED, PERFECT, PURE, LIGHT ENERGY OF LIMITLESS POWER AND POSSIBILITY. YOU ARE THE ONE WHO QUALIFIES THIS PURE AND PERFECT ENERGY AND DETERMINES HOW IT SHOWS UP IN THE PHYSICAL REALITY AROUND YOU.**

Here's a common analogy to explain this concept: Imagine that your life is a movie playing out on the screen in front of you in an old-timey movie theater that still uses film reels and light to project the picture. Source is the light. The light is the same no matter what film is playing on the reel. Everyone has equal access to this pure, perfect light to create whatever you wish on the screen of your life. You, however, are in control of what film is on the reel being projected on the screen. The film on the reel is your consciousness and it's projecting exactly what you think and believe about yourself and about life and the world.

If you believe with absolute certainty that life is a dog-eat-dog world of scarcity and competition filled with random illness, disease, fear, and selfish, hateful people—*that's what you experience*.

If you believe with absolute certainty that life is a joyous dance with the Divine, full of love, joy, vibrant health, abundance, and creativity leading you to your highest fulfillment and destiny—*that's what you experience*.

Neville Goddard explains it perfectly, "Consequently, what appears to you as circumstances, conditions, and even material objects is really only the product of your own consciousness."[3]

Are you starting to see just how powerful you are and just how much control you have over your life? You are the one who is choosing the scenes on the reel that's playing on the screen.

And what's more, you are the one who decides what role you play in that movie.

Are you the awesome hero who is helping to save the world? Or are you the fearful side character who lets everyone else decide for you what's happening in your life?

Are you the optimist who believes in herself and knows her life is working out fabulously? Or are you the bitter, resentful one stuck reliving the past and shutting out joy in the present?

**ONLY YOU CAN CHOOSE.**

Once you're conscious, awake, and aware of how much power you have and why your life is the way it is, you can start changing it. You decide who you're going to be. You decide which thoughts you think. You decide which emotions you focus on and cultivate. You decide what you believe. You decide what decisions you make. You decide what actions you take and how you react.

You are in control of *everything* that matters. You are a free-will being with untold and infinite power innate within you endowed by your Creator for you to use as you wish, in any way you want. Talk about incredible, right?

### Changing Your Consciousness—Who Do You Want to Be?

So, how do you change your consciousness, and therefore yourself and your life? You start with your thoughts.

Once upon a time, I was a corporate lawyer who worked on mergers and acquisitions and drafted and negotiated contracts. I hated my job and wanted a different life. But I didn't know what that different life looked like or what I wanted it to include. I had to figure it out for myself.

The first step to changing your consciousness is figuring out *who* you want to be and *what* you want your life to be like. If you don't know what you want, there's a 100 percent chance you might not get it.

You have to figure out what you do want before it can come into your reality. After all, your thoughts are the beginning of all creation, and if you don't know what you want to create, then how do you know what thoughts to think?

There are many ways you can go about figuring out what you want, but it seems like a safe bet to start with some basic questions that can lead you in the right direction:

> **How do you want to feel?**
> **What do you value?**
> **What do you enjoy?**
> **What makes you happy?**

As you can tell, only you can answer these questions for yourself. No one else, not even all the expensive life coaches in the world, can tell you what's in your heart of hearts, and that's the only place you're going to find these answers. But to find them, you have to spend time thinking about the questions. Shut off the distractions, break out a journal or a scratch pad, and then give yourself some time to dream.

> **Who do you want to be?**
> **What do you want to do?**
> **What do you want your life to include?**
> **What sounds like fun to you?**
> **What gets you excited?**

The possibilities are limitless. You have every option in the Universe available to you, even if you don't totally believe that yet. But for the purposes of this exercise, whenever you choose to do it, remove the limits. Because truly, the only person who puts limits on your life and the experiences you could have is *you*.

This is the first step to intentionally designing who you're becoming, and ultimately, your life—by thinking about it first. Everything starts as a thought, including your best life. It doesn't happen by accident. It doesn't happen *to* you. It happens *through* you.

Here are some other helpful questions you might use to figure out what you want to do or experience in your life, if you don't know already:

**What did you like to do as a kid?**
**What makes you lose track of time while you're doing it?**
**What feels like play to you?**
**What is fun for you?**
**What gives you joy?**

Bottom line: It all starts and ends with you and figuring out who you want to be and what kind of life you want.

**DON'T BE AFRAID TO THINK BIG.**
**LIKE, REALLY, REALLY BIG—NO MATTER YOUR AGE.**

Throw off all limits. Let yourself really dream—even if it's stuff you'd be embarrassed to admit you're dreaming about right now.

The plan the Universe has for you is so much grander and more incredible than anything you can imagine right now. It would blow your mind if you realized what was truly possible for you in this lifetime. Your wildest and most fanciful dreaming still may never be able to outdo what God can dream up for you. You might as well reach for the sky and let the Universe know that you're open to the most amazing, awesome, fulfilling life available to you.

Also, and this is important—don't share all your brand-new dreams for your future with just anyone and everyone you know. Keep them to yourself for a while. More on this soon.

**How We Radically Changed Our Consciousness**

**Jake**

While an F5 tornado destroyed a mile-wide stretch through the middle of his town, Jake didn't know whether he'd live or die as he sat in a small bathroom with a door breaking over his back. As the tornado roared overhead, Jake realized that if he died, his tombstone would only read *Son*. He realized he hadn't done anything in his life that would be remembered. It was a life-altering realization that shifted how Jake thought about himself and his life.

In that moment, he changed.

As he began to put his life back together after Mother Nature quite literally ripped it apart, Jake was a different person, on a different path.

He didn't know who he wanted to be or what he wanted to do, but his intuition told him to double down on doing something he loved, and he listened to it. For Jake, that something he loved was lifting weights. Working out had been his passion since high school, but it hadn't seemed like a likely career path or something that could lead to one.

But after that tornado tore apart his house and his life, he put his focus on doing what he loved and decided to see where it led. He changed who he was being by entering and preparing for his first bodybuilding competition.

Jake took the word *can't* out of his vocabulary. He became 100 percent positive, with an *I can do anything* attitude. He changed how he talked to himself in his head, and he changed how he talked about himself to other people. He wasn't just competing in a bodybuilding competition. In Jake's mind, he was *winning it*. And he told everyone that.

It was the predominant thought in his mind all day, every day throughout his prep. The certainty. The conviction. The show was as good as won, and he *knew it*.

He wrote words of encouragement on Post-it notes and stuck them everywhere, telling him he could do it and reminding him that he was unstoppable. He trained, he dieted, and he even did the things he hated—like cardio and eating boatloads of broccoli.

Jake became a different person because of the tornado—because he changed the story about himself in his head and unknowingly changed his consciousness. Jake wasn't the guy looking for a fight or getting hammered at the bar anymore. He became the guy who was *winning* this bodybuilding competition and trying to help others.

## CHANGING WHO HE WAS IN HIS MIND CHANGED *EVERYTHING*.

Jake won the bodybuilding show—his class and overall—and became a nationally qualified physique competitor. New opportunities opened up for him all over the place. Doubling down on something he loved ultimately led him on a completely different path—to a life beyond his wildest dreams.

If you ask him, he'll tell you that he didn't know a life this amazing was even possible.

But it is.

And to experience it, all he had to do was take a chance on himself, change who he was being, and remain open to all the possibilities the Universe had in store for him.

Jake didn't set out to become an internationally recognized tattoo and fitness model the day of that tornado. It just happened because he changed his consciousness. He changed what he thought and believed about himself. He changed the story in his head. He changed the story about what was possible for him. He made different choices that aligned with this new version of himself, and then his whole life path changed.

Thankfully, his path intersected with mine years later, planned and orchestrated to perfection by the very hand of God. More on that later.

### Meggan

My radical shift in consciousness happened in the basement of an office building, at a women's leadership class when I participated in an exercise called "True Values." In the midst of it, my heart cracked open and tears welled in my eyes as I realized my career as an attorney—the one I'd spent so much time, energy, and money to achieve—did not and never would align with my values.

That realization rocked me to the core.

With no idea what else I wanted to be, I felt lost. I spent months thinking about it, reading books about possible jobs for people with law degrees, applying for jobs that I never got interviews for, and then I finally figured out what I wanted in my life.

I wanted to be happy.

I wanted to be excited to wake up every morning and do something I loved. I wanted to have fun. I wanted to be healthy. I wanted to be fit. I wanted the freedom to choose how I spend my time every day, instead of being told how to spend it. I wanted to read and to create. I wanted to travel and see the world.

I tried on different possibilities in my mind—college professor, jewelry designer, entrepreneur, and writer . . . since I was still working on the book I'd started nearly two years earlier, but had no idea how to finish.

I even went so far as to design and make enough jewelry to launch an Etsy store that never went live, because something in me just wouldn't let me take that final step.

Then the law firm I had dedicated my life to for seven years caught wind of the fact that I didn't exactly want to be a lawyer anymore. I remember walking into my associate review, and the first words out of the partner's mouth were, "So, I understand you don't want to be a lawyer anymore."

My gut hit the floor.

At the time, it felt like the greatest betrayal of my life. I had shared my dreams with someone who I assumed had broken my confidence and told the partner. But it ended up being one of the greatest gifts I've been given by the Universe, because that's how these things work sometimes.

I couldn't bring myself to lie and say I wanted to be a lawyer, which is what the partner wanted to hear. Something inside me had shifted since that basement leadership group meeting, and the words wouldn't pass my lips.

Because I refused to say all the right things that would have protected the career I'd spent over a decade on, the firm gave me six months to decide if I still wanted to be a lawyer—or find a new job. Generous, really, in hindsight. Even more generous was the career coach they paid for who ended up being an angel in my life.

In one of our meetings, I told my new career coach about the book I was writing, and she changed my life with the words, "Set a deadline and finish the book."

Finish the book? I must have looked terrified. At that point, becoming a full-time author was still a pipe dream to me.

But I did it.

I set a deadline to finish the book and lined up a professional editor. And all of a sudden, in my head, I went from being a burned-out lawyer on the verge of losing her job to an aspiring author who was finishing her first book . . . for real. Then, everything started to change—because I had changed my self-concept. I had changed my consciousness.

You'd better believe, though, at that point I had *no idea* I would end up with titles gracing the *New York Times, Wall Street Journal, USA Today*, and international best-selling lists over *fifty times*. Or that I'd end up making millions doing something I loved that led me to my soul mate and the very best days of my life.

All I did was set a deadline and change the story about myself in my head. Then, I finished the book.

Bottom line: right now, in this moment, you do *not* know what is possible for you. But you can start figuring it out by deciding what you want and taking a step toward it. That's the first requirement for letting the Universe work some awesome magic in your world.

## Attention and Energy

Your attention is one of the most highly sought-after commodities in the world. It's in such high demand that companies spend billions every year to capture it. Crazy, right?

What you place your attention on is extremely important. Wherever you place your attention, you are directing your energy.

### WHERE ATTENTION GOES, ENERGY FLOWS.[4]

The longer you focus on something, the more energy you're giving it. Whatever your attention is focused on, you are feeding and causing to grow and expand in your world.

When I decided I wanted to become an author so I'd never have to negotiate another indemnity clause for the rest of my life, I gave it a *lot* of energy. I thought about it for hours throughout the day and at night. I dreamed about it, daydreamed about it, and envisioned what it would be like to love what I did. I imagined what it would be like to get up and do something every day that filled me with excitement and got me out of bed ready to take on the world. Every night as I fell asleep, I introduced myself to imaginary people as an author over and over again in my head, silently and steadily.

Just like Jake and his changed attitude, thoughts, positive self-talk, and reaffirming Post-it notes, I had no idea this was an actual method for changing my life and becoming who I wanted to be. None. I had no idea I was changing my consciousness. I didn't know anything about consciousness. I did it completely by accident. I had no idea why it worked. It took years before I realized why—which I never would have figured out if not for Jake's incredible intuition and insight.

We had both changed our lives by changing ourselves and the parallels between our experiences were obvious and numerous as we discussed them in greater and greater detail.

When we came to the conclusions you're reading about in this book, we knew we had to share them so other people could benefit from what we'd learned through our own experiences and research.

Doing what we both did isn't hard and it's not complicated, but it takes consistent effort to keep your thoughts and attention focused on what you want, as opposed to what most people focus their thoughts and attention on—what they don't want. Or alternatively, stuff that doesn't really matter and isn't helping take them anywhere great in life—like TV, video games, streaming content, social media, mass media, porn, gossip, celebrity culture, sports, family drama, hating their body, worrying about paying the bills, and fearing that the world is going to crap, etc.

Dr. Joe Dispenza explains why this kind of use of your attention is not wise:

> When your attention, and therefore your energy, is divided between all these outer-world objects, people, problems, and issues, there's no energy for you to put on your inner world of thoughts and feelings. So there's no energy left for you to use to create something new.[5]

Thankfully, you decide where your attention goes, and you can be very mindful about where you focus it.

We know this is the point where you may say that you don't have a choice about where your attention is focused all the time.

We get it. We all have different circumstances and situations.

I was once a corporate lawyer whose days were largely centered around drafting and negotiating contracts. I truly never wanted to draft or negotiate another contract for the rest of my life, and yet I would get up the next day and do it all over again.

*I made the choice to go to work the next day.* No one drove me to work at gunpoint and forced me to draft or negotiate contracts.

I drove there, sat at my desk, and stared at that computer all by myself. I did it because I had a mortgage and bills to pay, and I didn't know what else I was capable of doing. I let my fear of not being able to pay my mortgage dictate where my attention went, even if I didn't enjoy it.

Regardless of how much you do or do not like the choices you're currently making, it is an unavoidable truth that you are making them, even if it's choosing not to choose. That's still a choice.

You always have a choice. It may not be an easy one or an enjoyable one, but you get to choose. In fact, according to Dr. Hawkins, "[T]he only true freedom in the universe is the freedom of choice, which is the gift received by mankind."[6]

## YOU ARE A FREE-WILL BEING.
## WHEN YOU BECOME INTENTIONAL ABOUT WHERE YOU
## FOCUS YOUR ATTENTION, YOU CHANGE YOUR LIFE.

Why? Because you're changing your consciousness. Now you're a person who cares about where you place your attention.

What you focus your attention on gains energy and expands in your life. Focus it on things you want to give your energy to and have expand in your life.

One of the most important decisions I made happened in 2014. I quit watching TV. Cold turkey. Just *stopped*. I knew that if I wanted to become a full-time author and quit being a lawyer, I had to write books. Every moment that I focused my attention on TV, I wasn't focusing it on following my dreams. As much as I enjoyed watching *NCIS* reruns and every *CSI* spin-off, it was never going to write me a book. So, I quit.

I had *no idea* how life-changing that decision would turn out to be until years later. But I knew then, in my gut, that watching TV for hours every day was never going to get me closer to happiness and living the life of my dreams. In order to do that, I would have to put my attention and energy on doing everything in my power to help it happen.

Where attention goes, energy flows.[7] I stopped giving my attention and energy to TV and started focusing it on my own work that would make my dreams come true—a*nd they did.*

You can allow companies to spend billions attracting your attention, focusing your concentration, feeding off your energy, and evoking the emotions *they* want to evoke from you. This ultimately affects your consciousness and allows someone else to control your life experience. Is that what you want? Or do you want to be the one in control of your destiny?

Only you can decide and only you can change it.

# FOUR
## WORDS ARE POWERFUL

*The words you speak become the house you live in.*
*– Hafiz*

Your words matter. By this point in the book, you may not be too surprised by that. After all, everything about you matters.

Your words are an extension of your thoughts. They are verbalized, and sound carries vibration. As we've already discussed, vibration is really, really important in this energetic universe of ours.

You've probably heard the phrase *sticks and stones can break my bones, but words can never hurt me*. Jake and I often landed on this phrase as a point of contention. He maintained words couldn't hurt and you should never let them get to you, whereas I, as an author, said that words were really powerful. Turns out, we were both right. If you don't attach to or accept what someone says to you, their words can't hurt you. However, words are powerful in their own right.

As Florence Scovel Shinn, a brilliant metaphysician from the 1920s, points out in her wonderful work *Your Word is Your Wand*: "Jesus Christ emphasized the power of the word; 'By thy words thou shalt be justified and by thy words thou shalt be condemned,' and 'death and life are in [the] power of the tongue.'"[1]

Ernest Holmes goes further:

> Our word has the exact amount of power that we put into it. This does not mean power through effort or strain but power through absolute conviction, or faith…. We speak into our words the intelligence which we are, and backed by that greater intelligence of the Universal Mind our word becomes a law unto the thing for which it is spoken.[2]

If you constantly talk about tough financial times, how hard things are, how poorly things are going, how you're broke or sick, how much you hate your job or whatever, you're feeding more of your energy to those exact things you're speaking about. All this does is reaffirm that the things you do not want will continue to appear in your life. When you speak of being grateful, happy, healthy, beautiful, fortunate, lucky, wealthy, and joyful, you're also reaffirming more of those circumstances in your life.

You may have already guessed why that is, based on the earlier words of Dr. Joseph Murphy, but Florence is going to tell you again anyway. "Man has ever a silent listener at his side—his subconscious mind. Every thought, every word is impressed upon it and carried out in amazing detail."[3] Florence's stated goal was to "show how man can *change* his *conditions by changing his words*."[4]

According to Florence, who published *The Game of Life and How to Play It* in 1925, "Any man who does not know the power of the word, is behind the times."[5]

So, why is it that all these years later, people are still talking about being broke and sick and doing poorly, and therefore causing those conditions to continue to manifest in their lives? Because many still do not know the power of the word—or the power of the subconscious mind that's listening to every word we speak.

I know Florence is correct about the power of words because

I've experienced their power myself. I used to do something that I had no idea was so powerful, but in hindsight I've realized it has been one of the most influential means I've used to achieve pretty much every single goal I've ever had.

**I USED MY WORDS.**

It started when I was in college and I knew I wanted to go to law school. I used to sit alone in my room and introduce myself to imaginary people.

"Hi, I'm Meggan. I'm a law student."

I did this a lot. Not always out loud. Many times silently. Sometimes as I was falling asleep, like I mentioned before.

But the important thing was that I did it, and I did it because I was excited about who I was going to become. I was excited about becoming Meggan the law student. And eventually, I became Meggan the law student, sitting alone in my law-school dorm room, introducing myself to more imaginary people as Meggan the attorney. When I picked out the firm I *had to have a job at*, I added the name of the firm to my imaginary introduction.

And then a few years after I got the job at that firm, when I realized it was never going to make me happy, I started new imaginary introductions of myself that I was wildly excited about.

"Hi, I'm Meggan. I'm an author."

And it happened.

Then, "Hi, I'm Meggan. I'm a full-time author."

And it happened.

Then, "Hi, I'm Meggan. I'm a *New York Times* best-selling author."

And it happened.

You may sense a theme, I'm guessing.

**WORDS ARE POWERFUL.**
**WORDS ABSOLUTELY HAVE THE POWER TO CHANGE YOUR LIFE.**

How you use your words is deciding the course and quality of your life right now.

> **If you want to be wealthy, don't ever talk about being broke. Ever. Never. For real. Never.**
> **If you want to be healthy, don't ever talk about being sick. Never ever.**
> **If you want to be fit, don't ever talk about yourself as being fat or out of shape.**

It's the same as we covered with your thoughts. Choose them wisely. Be relentless about watching your words and your thoughts. They may be free, but they are not cheap. They never return void.

Words can also be powerful in a destructive fashion. I didn't know how much until I read *The Four Agreements* by don Miguel Ruiz. In the Toltec tradition (Toltec meaning "women and men of knowledge"[6]), "the first agreement is to *be impeccable with your word*."[7] Ruiz writes:

> Why your word? Your word is the power that you have to create. Your word is the gift that comes directly from God . . . Through the word you express your creative power. It is through the word that you manifest everything. Regardless of what language you speak, your intent manifests through the word . . .
>
> The word is not just a sound or a written symbol. The word is a force; it is the power you have to express and communicate, to think, and thereby to create the events in your life. You can speak. What other animal on the planet can speak? The word is the most powerful tool you have as a human; it is the tool of magic. But like a sword with two edges, your word can create the most beautiful dream, or your word can destroy everything around you.[8]

Ruiz adds, "All the magic you possess is based on your word. Your word is pure magic, and misuse of your word is black magic."[9]

When Ruiz dropped the bomb that gossip is "the worst form of black magic" and "pure poison," [10] I knew I had to quit gossiping. It was trickier than I thought it would be, and resulted in the loss of friends that I didn't expect to lose. But in hindsight, I can see that the decision to quit gossiping was a massive turning point in my life.

We highly recommend adding *The Four Agreements* to your reading list.

## WORDS ARE POWERFUL.
## BE CAREFUL HOW YOU USE THEM.

As Hafiz said at the beginning of this chapter, "The words you speak become the house you live in."

You hold creative power in your tongue. Create wisely.

### The Most Powerful Words

There are certain words that are *really, really* powerful. Especially these two:

### I AM.

"I AM" are two of the most powerful words you will ever speak. Anything you put after them, you are, or you are in the process of becoming. This is why you should never speak about yourself as being anything other than exactly what you want to be.

When you use the words "I AM" you are setting into motion the entire creative force of the Universe. When you say "I AM," you are acting as God of your Universe, decreeing something to come into existence. If you want to experience joyful outcomes, you will always speak these words with care and intention. Otherwise, who knows what you're creating?

**WHAT YOU SAY MATTERS.**

What you say about yourself matters the most for shaping your future. You should never speak anything after the words "I AM" that you do *not* want to become or bring into your world. For best results, use all "I AM" statements with wisdom and intention. They absolutely have the power to change your life.

Only you get to decide the words you speak. Decide wisely.

# FIVE
## WRITING YOUR OWN STORY

> No man ever steps in the same river twice,
> for it's not the same river and he's not the same man.
>
> – Heraclitus

When you grasp the power of consciousness and how it affects everything, you can look back over your life with fairly decent hindsight and see how who you were being and how you were thinking, speaking, and acting at the time created and attracted the situations, circumstances, experiences, and people into your world.

If you were expressing the consciousness of victimhood, then you might have found yourself in a situation where you felt victimized. If you were expressing the consciousness of lack, you might have found yourself broke. If you were expressing the consciousness of faith, you might have found yourself experiencing miracles.

Oftentimes, the hardest part is accepting our own role in creating the circumstances in our world. But when you grasp what it truly means, it's actually thrilling.

"What really frightens people about spiritual reality is that it confronts one with the reality that their destiny is solely within the power of their own hands. Heaven, like hell, is the result and consequence of one's own choices," says Dr. Hawkins in *Truth vs. Falsehood.*[1]

We hold that there's no reason to be frightened, but instead *empowered*.

## YOU ARE IN CONTROL.

If you don't like where you are now, you're the only one who can truly change it.

It's a process of releasing of who you are currently being in favor of becoming the person you want to be. It's the evolution of *you*, and it's the most important journey you're ever going to take in this life.

There's no one to blame or shame if you haven't gotten things right up to this point. In fact, it's wise to do the exact opposite. When you realize you are the architect and creator of all the situations and circumstances in your life—good and bad—you can begin to change them.

*This* is the empowering realization the awakened ones make.

We are not powerless pawns being swept along into the muddle of our destiny. No, we are the masters of our fates and captains of our souls, paraphrasing poet William Ernest Henley. We have free will, regardless of how divinely guided we are at every moment. Our free will is expressed through the decisions we make every day, all day long. And those decisions change our lives because they are an expression of our consciousness.

After Jake and I fell down the rabbit hole of quantum physics and the true nature of reality, we began to see life so differently. Instead of thinking of our decisions as meaningless, we realized that every decision you make is the equivalent of stepping onto a different timeline in the multiverse.

One decision can change the course of your entire life—like Jake's decision to enter the bodybuilding competition or my decision to set a deadline to finish my first book. But it's not only the big decisions that matter. The little decisions matter too. Each decision you make is an expression of your consciousness and is co-creating your life experience. Only you get to decide which timeline you're stepping onto in each moment.

Open your mind for this one:

**EVERY NOW-MOMENT IS HAPPENING SIMULTANEOUSLY. THERE IS NO FUTURE AND THERE IS NO PAST. THERE IS ONLY ONE INFINITE *NOW*.**

How can that be?
Time is a construct of man, as Jake loved to remind me when I used to worry about having enough time to finish a book before my deadline. Time and space are both constructs of man. They only exist in our minds and in the third-dimensional world as a result of the perfect out-picturing of our consciousness.

The truth is, even though you have calendars showing what you're doing next week and next year, you are living in the infinite now. This is why worry and anxiety about the past and future are truly useless. You are using the only moment in which you ever have the power to change anything, and you're filling it with fear or worry or stress or anxiety, attached to thoughts, which strengthens the energy behind them, making it more likely the things you're worrying about will be attracted into your life.

This is also why you're constantly told by the wise and spiritually advanced to *be present*. Many of us don't even know what that means.

What does it really mean?

**IT MEANS *YOUR ONLY POWER* IN THIS LIFETIME EXISTS IN THE PRESENT MOMENT.**

And what you do with this present moment, and all the other

now-moments that follow it, determines the course and trajectory of your life. It's not about what happened in the past. It's not even about what could happen in the future. It's about what you're doing in the *now*—in the present moment—that dictates your future.

### YOU CAN ONLY CHANGE YOUR LIFE IF YOU'RE PRESENT IN THE *NOW*.

If you choose to spend many of your now-moments with your eyes glued to a screen, being entertained and watching other people live their lives, the outcomes you experience will reflect that choice. Why? Because you've handed your power over to a screen. You're giving a screen your attention and your energy. Essentially, you trade the power to change your life for being entertained.

We are not saying all screen time or entertainment is bad. We're just pointing out that it's really important to be mindful about where you place your attention, and the benefit, or lack thereof, it has in your life.

As a lifelong reader, I have spent many tens of thousands of hours buried in books, living adventures in my mind that absolutely enlivened and enriched my life and helped me become the author I became, which led me to my soul mate. I could never say those hours were a bad investment, because I love the outcome they produced, and I'm eternally grateful for every single thing on my path because of where it led me.

But we all have to be aware of how we spend our now-moments, especially if you're spending as many as possible *escaping* from your current reality instead of *changing* your reality.

It's not a bad thing. Before you awaken, you escape. It's normal. But once you realize that you can change your reality and create one that's even better than your escape, it's game on.

The time you have on this Earth is precious. The clock is already ticking down to the end of your experience in this body, in this incarnation. You will never be exactly who you are in this moment, ever again. It's like the quote at the beginning of the chapter that I've loved for over twenty years—you will never be the same person as you are right now.

Your higher self—the infinite, eternal part of you—chose to incarnate on Earth at this time for a specific reason. Mystics say that Earth is an advanced spiritual school, and the opportunity to incarnate here is in high demand. That means the part of you that is one with Source chose to incarnate. Here. Now.

Your birth and life are no accident.

In fact, Dr. Hawkins proved through his consciousness research that "the particulars of *every* individual's birth are absolutely, perfectly karmically just and maximally advantageous, despite appearance or personal opinion to the contrary."[2]

You were meant to be born when you were born, where you were born, into the life and body you were born. There are no mistakes. Everything was perfectly decided prior to your incarnation to set you up for the maximum amount of soul growth in this lifetime, according to the karma you have accumulated over many, many lifetimes.

We are each Divinely guided in the unfoldment of our souls—if only we can shake the societal programming, conditioning, brainwashing, and demoralization we've been subjected to for most, if not all, of our lives. We are here to learn, grow, and evolve. To progress along our soul's curriculum over many lifetimes. Whether you believe in reincarnation or not, both it and the concept of karma calibrate as truth in Dr. Hawkins' consciousness research.[3] What's more, he's also found that the statement "the exact time of bodily 'death' is karmically set at birth" also calibrates as true.[4]

If you knew that your life circumstances weren't just some twist of fate and that you were here on purpose—with this personality and everything that goes with it—would it change how you felt about your life?

Only you can decide what you believe, but we find these truths proven by Dr. Hawkins to be empowering, helping us to be more fearless about becoming exactly who we are meant to become in this lifetime and to be more courageous about playing our role in the Divine Plan of love unfolding on this planet right now.

Only you get to choose what you accept as true. Why not believe everything is working out perfectly and in your best interest, regardless of outer appearances?

Remember that seeming betrayal I walked into during my associate review that turned out to be one of the greatest gifts I've ever received from the Universe?

There's a much larger plan in play, designed by the unknowable brilliance of Infinite Intelligence itself. It's so much bigger than any one of us, and yet, every single one of us is an inextricable and vital part of it. We are all here to play a role.

Certain aspects are already decided before you come into incarnation, but never forget you are a free-will being.

You get to choose.

In my mind, the Divine Plan is somewhat similar to the ever-evolving process I've used as a storyteller to plot and write dozens of awesome, twisty fictional stories. There are certain knowns for each plot. There are also certain big scenes that the storyteller knows will happen during the book. Big moments and turning points.

But then there's the entire rest of the book, and that is driven by the characters—not the author. I let the characters tell *me* how all the in-between parts go.

Some of the major life events you're going to experience have likely already been predetermined before your birth by the Divine Storyteller, but *you* get to dictate the rest as a free-will being. This is where your thoughts, words, beliefs, actions, reactions, and decisions all come in.

So, what kind of story are you living? Only *you* have the power to flip the script and create that epic next chapter.

# SIX
## FALLING IN LOVE WITH YOU

Self-love is the key that opens the door. You cannot hate your way into anything good, but you can love yourself into the life of your dreams.
– Meggan Wilson

Loving yourself unconditionally is the ultimate act of rebellion. Loving yourself is also key to becoming who you want to be and living a life that you love. What's more, loving yourself isn't just about you. It's actually good for everyone.

We've established that your consciousness is what creates the life you live, but it also affects every other person on the planet. Remember when we said that you matter? *You matter so much.*

**YOUR CONSCIOUSNESS AFFECTS *EVERYONE*.**

What's more, everyone else's consciousness affects you. That's because, as we covered earlier, *we're all one*. We all share one collective consciousness.

You know the quote, "*Be the change you wish to see in the world*"? It sounds like a cliché due to societal programming, but in it lies the simple wisdom of so many so-called clichés.

## WHEN YOU CHANGE, YOU CHANGE THE WORLD.

The happier and more delighted you are with yourself and your life, the better life gets on the planet for everyone. No matter what. Every time. You affect the collective consciousness when you change your individual consciousness.

The collective consciousness is the source of events that affect us all on a large scale. For instance, the state of world affairs, wars, mass shootings, etc. Those things can only happen on a planet with a collective consciousness that is made up of a lot of people who are a mess inside.

As within, so without—another Universal Law.

The work you do on yourself is beneficial for the entire collective. This is why it isn't selfish to work on yourself. It's actually the only sure way you can help save the world, and only *you* can do it. When you raise your vibration, it affects everyone and everything. When you become a better, healthier, happier, more loving version of yourself, you change the world, and that leads to better outcomes for humanity.

Societal programming may have you thinking that it's selfish to spend time focusing on yourself, but nothing could be further from the truth. Let's revisit what selfishness really is.

## SELFISH CHOICES AND DESIRES ARE THOSE THAT ONLY BENEFIT *YOU* AND NO ONE ELSE.

Because you're connected to the rest of us, it's actually an act of love toward all humanity when you start becoming a better version of you and loving yourself more. This is changing the cause, instead of futilely trying to change the effects in the outside world.

If you want to start overhauling your life and becoming the person you want to become, you have to make new choices and create new habits that are in alignment with the future you want to experience.

Here are a few practices that you can incorporate into your life that can have massive effects, including increasing your capacity to love yourself more, just like they have for us.

### Gratitude

As Dr. Joe Dispenza stated in a video I once watched, "Gratitude is the ultimate state of receivership." The emotion of gratitude correlates to one of the highest, fastest vibrations of all emotions. When sustained, it attracts to you more situations, people, and experiences to be grateful about.

**GRATITUDE IS A MASTER KEY TO HAPPINESS.**

We've all heard it and it sounds like a cliché, but it's true: the more you count your blessings, the more blessings you have to count. Again, this is the Law of Attraction at work. Grateful people attract awesome reasons to be grateful. Think about it in your own daily life. Who do you do something extra for? The person who doesn't even bother to thank you? Or the person who is genuinely appreciative of your time, effort, and everything you do for them?

**GRATEFUL PEOPLE ATTRACT MORE
TO BE GRATEFUL FOR.**

Good news: gratitude is something you cultivate. You can start practicing gratitude wherever you are, exactly as you are. Anyone can do it, and it's free. Plus, it takes you to really amazing, wonderful places, and it makes all the things you already enjoy *even better*. Gratitude is magical.

Here are some easy ways to incorporate gratitude into your day that have the power to change your world:

## Wake Up Grateful

Change the first thought you have in the morning to one of gratitude.

As soon as you feel yourself starting to become conscious, start thinking about how grateful you are that you woke up, how grateful you are that you're alive, how grateful you are that today is a wonderful day, when miracles will happen. Feel the warmth in the center of your chest grow as you supercharge your day.

It wasn't until this book was almost finished that I learned Henry David Thoreau used to do something similar. Thoreau would "lie abed for awhile in the morning telling himself all the good news he could think of; that he had a healthy body, that his mind was alert, that his work was interesting, that the future looked bright, that a lot of people trusted him."[1] Then he'd get out of bed "to meet the day in a world filled for him with good things, good people, good opportunities."[2]

### HOW YOU WAKE UP MATTERS.

Do it with gratitude, instead of thinking about all the things you have to do, the things that stress you out, or how much you don't want to go to work. Waking up with gratitude has the power to change the trajectory of your entire day. Try it out for yourself.

## Fall Asleep Grateful

As you fall asleep at night, change your thoughts to ones of gratitude. Think of anything and everything you're grateful for. Again, feel the warmth in your chest grow as you raise your vibration and impress into the subconscious mind how grateful you are, so that it knows to send you more to be grateful for. Then you fall asleep happy and grateful. It's a great way to live.

*Keep a Gratitude Journal*

You can do your gratitude journaling in the morning, at night, throughout the day, or any combination that suits you. Journaling about the things you're grateful for requires you to think about what you're grateful for, which raises your vibration, fills you with warmth and love as you write it down, and—bonus—it keeps you on the lookout all day for things to write down that you're grateful for. Keeping a gratitude journal is a really easy way to brighten your life.

*Express Gratitude*

Express your gratitude to people for the things they do for you. Tell people you're grateful for them and their contributions to your life. Thank people. All the time. Express your gratitude to them, and really *feel* what you're saying. It's raising your vibration and your subconscious mind is listening.

*Accept Gratefully*

If you're given or offered something that you would normally say "oh no, you don't have to," or "oh no, I couldn't possibly," try gratefully accepting it. Many people who love to give have trouble receiving, and practicing receiving things gratefully can open up channels for the Universe to bring you even more wonderful gifts. Plus, you're giving other people a chance to give generously, and that makes them feel awesome too.

According to Florence, life is "a great game of *Giving and Receiving*" so make sure you're receiving gratefully too.[3]

*The Extreme Sport of Gratitude*

You can even turn gratitude into an extreme sport. If something adverse happens during your day, find some aspect of it to be grateful for or create a story around why you're grateful it happened. If you can find gratitude for something that's going wrong, *while it's going wrong*, you're doing awesome.

I once found massive gratitude in the middle of not being able to breathe. How? I realized in that moment that fear truly was not real, and the realization was incredibly powerful.

When I walked into that unventilated greenhouse, my lungs seized up and I couldn't get any breath into my body, but I felt *no fear*. I just reacted—perfectly. I realized in life-threatening situations, there's no fear. Fear is an illusion. That was also the exact moment I realized gratitude could be an extreme sport. I have a lot of gratitude for that unventilated greenhouse for teaching me this.

You can even take it a step further and find gratitude for all the worst things that have ever happened to you because of the lessons you learned from them and the way they changed your path through life. After years of grief, I was finally able to find gratitude for losing my father in a very sudden, very tragic fashion. He was killed in a fifteen-car pile-up on a snowy Michigan highway. He was the only one not to walk away. It shattered me, but it woke me up and made me realize that life was too short to be unhappy. Most of the best things in my life came as a result of that horrendous wake-up call. It was a life-defining moment that ultimately put me on the path to an existence so magical I didn't know it was possible. Being able to find gratitude for such a hard experience not only dissipated my grief, but gave me incalculable inner strength.

**WHEN YOU CAN FIND GRATITUDE FOR THE WORST THINGS THAT HAVE EVER HAPPENED TO YOU, YOU'RE ENTERING NEW AND UNCHARTED TERRITORY WHERE ANYTHING IS POSSIBLE.**

Gratitude truly has the power to change *everything* in your life. It's something you can only understand after you've experienced it for yourself. And just like everything else in this book, you have to *do* it yourself *for* yourself.

And above all, don't just count your blessings. Cherish them and give thanks for every step of the journey that brought you to where you are. Being grateful for the life you have leads to having an even better life to be grateful for.

**The Fine Art of Forgiveness**

The benefits of forgiveness cannot be overstated, and just like the benefits of gratitude, cannot truly be known until you've experienced them for yourself.

## WHO ARE WE FORGIVING AND WHY? ANYONE AND EVERYONE FOR ANYTHING AND EVERYTHING—INCLUDING YOURSELF.

For real. Forgive everyone. For everything. Including YOU. Forever.

Anything you're holding on to that causes hate, anger, judgment, resentment, shame, guilt, animosity, irritation, annoyance, jealousy, envy, or pain is negatively affecting your life, your body, your health, your happiness, and your future because it's negatively affecting your mental state, your emotions, your vibration, your thoughts, and your beliefs.

You've probably heard before that forgiveness isn't for the other person, and it's not. It's for you. It literally changes nothing for the other person—they probably won't even know that you forgave them—but it can change *your entire life* and your life's trajectory. Holding a grudge isn't a good thing, despite what societal conditioning has programmed into many people. Let it go. Let it *all* go. As Jake says, it's way easier to climb a ladder with two hands than with one hand on a rung and the other carrying a bag full of crap.

It doesn't matter how unforgivable you think what someone did was, or how long you've been holding on to it, or how terrible you believe what *you* did was—forgive them and forgive yourself. Literally as soon as you can possibly manage. If you knew how damaging it was to hold onto those kinds of thoughts and emotions, you would feel them as fast as possible and release them as fast as possible. You already know how you feel matters. Forgiveness will make you feel *amazing*. And if you can find gratitude for what you're forgiving, *you are a rock star!*

How do you get yourself across the bridge to be ready to forgive? Knowing these things can be really helpful:

- People simply speak, act and react from their level of consciousness. They can only be what they are. They don't know anything else. That's not something you can hold against anyone or yourself. You don't know what you don't know.
- It's not our place to judge. Judgment is a low-vibration emotion, and what's more, we can never know all the reasons why someone else does something, which means we never know the complete story. Only an omniscient being ever could. Plus, the laws of the Universe already have it covered. Source knows all, sees all, and is everywhere. People always reap what they sow. You don't need to get involved and lower your vibration. Karma already has it handled much better than you ever could.
- By holding on to things from the past, you're feeding them your vital energy and keeping those situations and thought forms alive. Where does that vital energy come from? As we discussed, that energy is draining out of your present moment, the only moment you have any power. Basically, by holding on to the past, you're selling out your awesome future. Let it go.

So, how do you actually forgive? This is the process we use, and it feels *amazing*. Massive thanks to John Randolph Price for writing the book *Living a Life of Joy*, because that's where we picked it up:

Imagine a fire burning within you—any color and any size. See it in your mind's eye. You can call it the Internal Fire, the Divine Flame, the Holy Fire within, or whatever you want to call it. The name doesn't matter, but what you do with the fire does. Now, bring a picture of the situation requiring forgiveness into your mind's eye. *Do not engage with the picture of the situation.* Don't relive it. Don't get caught up in the emotions. Just see it. Acknowledge it. And then throw the picture on the Holy Fire within, and watch it burn away and turn back into energy that releases like gold dust. Feel the physical release as you let it go, perhaps in your chest or shoulders. Feel the weight lift off your body. You can silently chant "I forgive you" or "I forgive myself" as it dissipates. Throw the picture of the situation or a word that represents it on the fire as many times as you need to until you forget about the situation entirely. If it ever pops back up in your mind, continue throwing it on the Holy Fire within and forgiving. Do it over and over again, if necessary, until one day, it just stops popping up.

Know that when you're doing this, you are under grace, and the forgiveness is complete in reality as soon as it's complete in your mind and heart. It's that easy. And it really makes a *massive* difference in your life and the joy you're capable of accessing.

Living light because you have no past baggage is a beautiful thing. Anyone and everyone can do it, and it's free. Anything you sincerely offer up to the Holy Fire within is extinguished through spiritual transmutation.

You can start right where you are, as you are, in this moment. You can do it right now.

Close your eyes. Envision the fire. Take your baggage and everything you're holding on to, all those grudges and grievances, and toss them one by one on the flames of the Holy Fire within to be transmuted. Feel the purity of your heart as the shame, rage, guilt, anger, self-condemnation, regret, and all the other negative emotions disappear into the flames.

You can do this all day, every day.

We constantly forgive ourselves for everything we've ever done, said, thought, and been, and then we forgive everyone else too. This practice is a regular staple in our lives and has made a massive difference.

You can also let go of all the crap from your day each night before you go to bed too. Once you're in the habit, it gets quicker and easier. It really works.

Sometimes, forgiving other people can be easier than forgiving yourself. But it's massively important to forgive yourself fully too. Even if you think you deserve the punishment of holding onto whatever you've said or done—you don't. It doesn't matter what it was. Truly. You can be forgiven in an instant. All it takes is *wanting* to let it go.

## FORGIVE YOURSELF.

If you can look upon the memory and see only the wisdom the situation brought you or taught you without a negative emotional reaction, you're there.

And if you keep getting tripped up on the same situation or guilt or shame, *keep forgiving yourself.* Over and over again until you can do it sincerely and surrender the burden you've been carrying for far too long. Let it go. You will become a better person because of it. You don't need to be punished any longer. You hold the keys to release yourself from the prison you've locked yourself inside.

## LET IT GO.

If someone has really wronged you or treated you unfairly and it's causing you to get stuck in low-vibration negative emotions, forgive that person. Not for them, but for you.

You don't need to carry that burden. You'll soar without it.

Returning to where it feels good to live vibrationally is way more important than replaying how someone wronged you or let you down over and over again. Of course, you'd nail that argument if you had a do-over, but let it go anyway. Thinking about it is just feeding it energy and telling your subconscious that you want more people and situations in your life to give you the same feeling—which you certainly don't.

Inner peace is its own reward, and you have no idea how important or incredible it is until you experience it. It's like health or fitness or meditation or fearlessness. You cannot know how absolutely worth your effort they are until you personally experience the benefits. And then you can't imagine *not* living life that way.

The best things in life truly are free and available to you to start experiencing as soon as you decide you want to take the first step.

Living at a high vibration—feeling good emotions pretty much all the time—is an amazing way to live.

A beautiful mind makes it possible to have a beautiful life. And forgiveness is one powerful way to beautify your mind.

**Surrender**

Surrender is a key that opens the door to a fearless, worry-free, and stress-free life. Surrender is *magical.* Again, it's free. Anyone can do it. It's easy. You can start doing it today, right now.

So, what exactly is surrender? Surrender is an act of faith, and faith is incredibly powerful. Wildly powerful. When you surrender something that's worrying you, stressing you out, or causing you anxiety, you are trusting that it's being worked out for your highest good by Infinite Intelligence, in accordance with the Divine Plan.

**SURRENDER IS YOUR CONSCIOUS CHOICE TO PUT YOUR ENERGY INTO FAITH RATHER THAN FEAR.**

## NOT RELIGION—*FAITH.*

Why would you want to do that? Because faith is empowering. Faith makes you powerful, poised, and peaceful. Fear is disempowering. Fear makes you weak, scared, timid, and easy to manipulate. Who would you rather be?

When you surrender your burden to Infinite Intelligence, you are opening yourself up to Divinely inspired solutions to anything you could possibly be facing, or for the burden to disappear completely without you having to do *anything at all.* It's actually really awesome.

So, how do you do it?

Remember the Holy Fire within? If that method works for you, it's your new best friend. You can use it for everything and anything. It's a quick and easy way to add immeasurable peace to your life. If something is going sideways, take a quick mental picture of the situation and toss it on the Holy Fire within. Let it burn away and reveal the beautiful energetic pattern behind it.

If you feel yourself start to worry, stress, or get anxious about the same situation, do it again. Throw it on the fire over and over until you can let it go and trust that it is being handled for you. Continuing to worry about it after you've surrendered is effectively telling the Universe that you'd rather freak out about it yourself instead of letting the Divine handle it for you.

Also, when you surrender, you're trusting that when and if there's something that you need to do personally, you'll know it and you'll be guided to do it.

Why would you want to surrender?

As you might have guessed, worrying about things and imagining all the ways something could possibly go wrong is the best way to impress your subconscious with all the pictures of what you don't want. That's pretty much the opposite track if you're trying to improve your life or invite good things into it. Stress, worry, anxiety, and fear all lower your vibration and lead to you attracting more things to stress about, worry about, be anxious about, and be fearful of. When you surrender, you are letting go and shortcutting right to feeling like everything is working out in your best interest.

Surrender is a practice, just like gratitude and forgiveness. For best results, do it all the time, with pretty much anything.

Like all of these tools, it may feel strange at first. But the more you do it, the better it feels and the better it works for you.

If at first you can't rid yourself of the nagging worries or fears, double down on your faith. You have to change your expectations and beliefs about life if you want to change your life. In order to receive the amazing things that are on your Divine path, you have to expect amazing things and believe they are possible for you.

When you surrender a situation, you're essentially saying, "Okay, Infinite Intelligence, you do your part and I'll do mine. What I'm not going to do is worry about anything. I know that literally helps nothing and no one. By worrying, I would simply be investing my energy in fear over faith, which takes away my power and lowers my vibration, and I don't do that anymore."

Remember when we talked about Source being real and at work within you and around you all the time? This may feel like you're doing "nothing," but surrender is real. Your visualization of tossing the situation on the Holy Fire within actually has very real energetic effects that can liberate you from the bondage of whatever has you trapped in worry, fear, anxiety, or any other negative emotion. It actually works if you give it a chance.

Given the backward societal conditioning we've all experienced, it can sometimes be easier to go with fear over faith, but it's never the right choice. Ever. Fear is one of the lowest vibration emotions you can experience. It takes you to dark, dense, heavy places that do not have good outcomes for you or your life. Fear is literally inverted faith. You're putting all your chips on the table, betting that bad things are going to happen. Your subconscious is going to deliver what you expect. Why place your bets on fear when you can choose a different way?

Don't worry if it's hard to let go at first, and you still have nagging worries after you've surrendered. Just do it again and again until you can let it go and not think about the situation at all. Because as long as you're putting your energy into fear, you're preventing Infinite Intelligence from being able to come up with a genius solution for the greatest good.

You can cultivate faith if it's foreign to you. Lean into it, and it grows. You just have to—you guessed it—have faith.

# SEVEN
## KARMA, THE DIVINE PLAN, AND THE SAFETY SWITCH ON YOUR POWER

*Whatsoever a man soweth, that shall he also reap.*
— Galatians 6:7

Now that you're learning how powerful you are, you're probably ready to start unleashing that power so you can get on to living the life of your dreams as quickly as possible—which is fabulous! But before we move on to your greatest asset in creating a life you love, we need to talk about another important concept. Again, this is something you may have heard before:

**WITH GREAT POWER COMES GREAT RESPONSIBILITY.**

As you grow in consciousness, your power grows, and everything you do carries more weight. This means that as you understand how powerful your thoughts and words are, they actually become more powerful, and you need to be even wiser about how you use them. It's a little like a Kung Fu master not being able to start a bar fight without possibly greater repercussions if he hurts someone because of his years of training.

The Law of Karma is a real Universal Law, but it doesn't have to be scary. The Law of Karma is simply the law of cause and effect, constantly operating, that keeps perfect score and order in our world. The Law of Karma says that everything you to do to someone, you will experience in either this or another lifetime.

We all reap what we sow. It makes sense why many of us heard so much about the Golden Rule as kids: *do unto others as you would have done unto you.* That's because of the Law of Karma.

Every action you take, word you speak, and thought you think is pre-paving your future. Every moment you live isn't just receding into the past; it is springing forward to determine your future experiences. This is another reason why forgiveness is absolutely vital. Forgiveness offers you grace.

**Service-to-Self vs. Service-to-Others**

When you're figuring out what you want for your future, it's important to make sure that your desires are unselfish and harmless to you and all others.

You have two choices in life when it comes to picking teams, and you have to choose one. One choice is service-to-self. The other choice is service-to-others. That's it. Dark or light. Those are your two choices. Choose wisely who you're going to serve.

If you're like us, you've probably made some service-to-self choices in your life. And like us, you might have realized that they didn't ultimately take you anywhere good or if they did, it wasn't the experience you thought you were signing up for.

Here's where it gets serious. Using your power to manifest purely selfish desires—desires that are purely service-to-self—is black magic.[1] The outcome of manifesting selfish desires can be very destructive and unpleasant for you to experience. We're only about white magic in this book and in our lives, so avoiding the manifestation of purely selfish desires—which benefit only you and *no one else*—is a very safe and sane way to operate.

How do you know if a desire is selfish? One quick way to check is to ask yourself whether what you want is constructive or destructive. Destructive desires are selfish. Constructive desires are not.

A few questions to ask yourself:

> **Am I trying to take something away from someone else?**
> **Am I trying to manifest something that doesn't belong to me?**
> **Will anyone be harmed by the manifestation of this desire?**
> **Does this desire benefit only me and no one else?**

If you're answering yes to any of those questions, then attempting to bring such a thing into your life will undoubtedly bring negative consequences that could likely be very unpleasant to experience, if not downright painful and devastating.

We know. We've done it. We'll never do it again.

But you are a free-will being, and Source is so generous that It will allow you to misuse the powers It has endowed you with to your heart's content. But don't be surprised if your life turns into Hell on Earth as a result.

We're not saying this to scare you, but to help you realize how much power your free will provides you with. You can do whatever you want with it. That's the freedom that God has given you. You determine whether you make your life Heaven or Hell—and only you can decide.

Many books will tell you that you can have literally whatever you want—which you can—but some neglect to mention that you don't necessarily want to manifest everything and anything you've ever dreamed of in your life.

As we've mentioned throughout the book, there is a Divine Plan, orchestrated by Infinite Intelligence, that is unfolding at every moment. You are part of this Divine Plan. Your birth, the family you were born into, and everything else about you is enmeshed in the

Divine Plan. For best results, you only want to manifest things in line with the Divine Plan.

And before you start thinking that whatever you've picked out for yourself is better than anything the Divine Plan could ever deliver to you, know that God has such an incredible, amazing, unbelievably awesome plan for you personally that you can't even begin to fathom it right now. We speak from personal experience. Neither of us could have possibly imagined a life so wonderful as the one we have now, and we didn't get here alone. God's hand was in every single part that turned out awesome.

Here's the CliffsNotes version of one example: I pinned a picture on a Pinterest board for a hero I was preparing to write. I searched for a sexy tattooed man, and what came up was the most beautiful headless picture of a man I'd ever seen. He had a body that looked like it was carved by the hand of a master, and the most entrancing tattoos.

When I pinned his picture, I had no idea that I was pinning the picture of my future husband. There was *no way* on God's green Earth that I could have *ever* imagined that a guy who looked like that would fall in love with me—or that he'd have a heart of gold and a consciousness of health that would change my life in miraculous ways. I would never have dared to *dream* such a thing, let alone actually think that it could happen. Plus, I'd sworn to myself that I was going to stay single for five years after my divorce.

But the Universe had a way better plan for me. The Universe had planned Jake for me.

Almost a year after I pinned the picture, through the most serendipitous circumstances, we met. Years later, he told me he knew that day that I was the one.

I was still in shock that the guy from Pinterest was even *real*—and even better in the flesh than what I could write about in a book. Not to mention that it was possible for him to be so nice and normal that he even impressed my mother to the point where *she* was the one talking about him when I was walking away still stunned from our first meeting.

A few months later, we moved in together on the beach in Belize, and a couple of years after that, we eloped in a fairy-tale wedding in Fiji.

We have had many life experiences that have shown us without a doubt that Source is real, God loves us unconditionally, and the Divine Plan is so *freaking awesome* that we never could have imagined how incredible it could be. Infinite Intelligence has an amazingly awesome plan for you too. Pretty cool, don't you think?

So, how do you know what's in line with the Divine Plan? Any unselfish, constructive desire that you have. Constructive is defined as: "leading to improvement; positive."[2]

And before you start to worry that the money you may want to manifest might fall under the category of selfish, don't. It isn't. Infinite Intelligence understands that you need money to live in this reality at present and wants you to have an abundance of it. Your financial freedom is absolutely in line with the Divine Plan. You can play a bigger and more useful role in the Divine Plan when all your energy isn't sucked up by just trying to pay the bills and get by.

You being vibrantly healthy is also totally in line with the Divine Plan. And so is you experiencing unconditional love. There are an infinite number of constructive desires that align with the Divine Plan. Remember, anything that causes you to become a better version of yourself positively impacts the entire human collective and helps change the world for the better. That's constructive. That's a gift to humanity.

Plus, the more you grow in consciousness, the more you will realize that you only want things that are in line with the Divine Plan. You don't want anything that could possibly be selfish or harm someone else. It's just not worth it, and the damage it can cause and the karma it can carry . . . you don't even want to contemplate it.

Thankfully, for all our benefit, Infinite Intelligence has installed a safety switch on our power. That safety switch is *love*. Brilliant, right? Not that we would expect anything less from the omniscient, omnipotent, omnipresent Creator of the Universe.

## YOU CAN'T EXERCISE YOUR INFINITE POWERS WITHOUT DOING IT *WITH LOVE*.

In order to bring a manifestation into being, you have to be able to pour love from your heart onto a mental picture of it. Love is the operating force behind all manifestation.

Your power can only grow to a certain level without unconditional love. This is as it should be. Until you can operate from unconditional love, full dominion over the vast powers of the Universe are denied to you for your own good.

You wouldn't hand a flamethrower to a three-year-old, would you? It's the same with us. Infinite Intelligence knows better than to give us a chance to burn the whole planet down by accident. It should. It knows each of us intimately.

The more you learn, grow, and evolve on your path, the more you will realize that everything about each of us has been designed perfectly, including this.

So, who was the last human we know of to achieve full dominion and mastery over the powers of the Universe?

Jesus Christ.[3]

There's a reason everyone knows His name. While a deep discussion of this topic is beyond the purview of this particular book, you should know that Jesus Christ was the first Christian metaphysician. His miracles were simply demonstrating the laws of the Universe in action, and Jesus isn't the only one capable of doing seemingly miraculous things. We all have access to the same power.

It starts to make sense why Jesus said to pray for and bless your enemies, because He knew the rules to the game of life and how to apply them.

Bottom line:

**MORE FAITH AND MORE LOVE IS ALWAYS THE RIGHT ANSWER WHEN YOU'RE CREATING THE LIFE OF YOUR DREAMS.**

# EIGHT
## HELPING YOUR DREAMS COME TRUE

> Imagination is the beginning of the growth of all forms, and faith is the substance out of which they are formed.
> – Neville Goddard

Your imagination is your greatest super power. Who would've guessed? It makes sense that Jesus said, "Become as little children."[1] Kids are really good at this stuff, because honestly, it's probably all supposed to be *taught to children*. Jake and I believe that's why all of these concepts are really quite simple. Kids have to be able to understand it. But regardless of whether we were supposed to be taught this at a much younger age, we're learning them now.

Your imagination, when you use it constructively, is you being God picturing the plan for your life and your future. We know this is true because we've used our imaginations to achieve every single thing we've accomplished in this life.

Jake uses his imagination extensively in sculpting his body. It wasn't just hours in the gym and eating clean that created his physique. It was constantly envisioning himself in his head as an action figure, like the ones he played with as a kid—and he's been doing it since he was a kid! Is it any wonder he looks like a literal superhero? No, not at all. Because that's how he sees himself in his head.

Now do you believe this works? We hope so, because it does.

I used to constantly imagine myself as a lawyer, and then as an author, and now . . . well, I'm keeping what's next a secret.

## When Secrets Are Good

This brings us to an important point mentioned before that deserves further discussion.

Whatever it is that you want to bring into your life—whatever that desire is in your heart of hearts—keep it a secret. The powers you have are wildly powerful, but you have to use them wisely, and that includes using them quietly.

Why? Because if you go around telling everyone about all of your new beloved dreams and the incredible future that you're co-creating, you're going to encounter what is commonly referred to as mass consciousness or the race mind.

What is that? It's the consciousness of everyone who doesn't believe this stuff is possible. It's doubt. Disbelief. Fear. Judgment. Snide comments that will hammer and chisel away at your certainty that this newly formed dream is actually coming true.

Until you have so much conviction in your heart and soul—until you *know* down to the marrow of your bones with absolute certainty that no one can sway you from your belief about what is manifesting in your life—those hammers and chisels can kill your dream dead.

More beautiful futures and wondrous creations have been destroyed by sharing a dream too soon than you can possibly imagine. In fact, it's often the people closest to you who are most likely to kill the dream before it can come into manifestation. These people can even be very well-meaning, but they generally don't have a problem with telling you all the reasons why what you want isn't possible, why it won't work out, or why there's no chance it could happen for you.

Some people love to point out all the pitfalls and potential issues you're going to face. They might tell you how it's such a long shot or a pipe dream or too unrealistic. They may just be scared because they don't want you to change, and you creating your awesome new future is definitely going to result in change.

Every single one of these comments is absorbed by your subconscious, and you don't want or need their doubt, fear, and negativity imprinting upon you.

Another reason to keep your dreams a secret: people may constantly ask you how it's going during the process, bringing your attention to the fact that what you want hasn't manifested in your life yet. This is absolutely something you don't want.

Thinking about why you don't have the reality of your dream yet is a surefire way to push the manifestation further away from you because you're focusing on the *lack* of what you want instead of *what you want*. It's a subtle difference of where you put your attention, but it's a crucial one.

One of the most important decisions I intuitively made in my life was not telling many people about my big dream of becoming a full-time author. Sure, I told some people—a few family members and a few friends who I thought would be excited about it and supportive of me. And they were, mostly. Although, some were extremely skeptical.

Thankfully, I didn't care. I *knew* that I was meant to go into the business of publishing and become a full-time author, and I knew it with such deep conviction that they couldn't sway me.

When I took a new job and moved across the state in the midst of trying to make this big dream come true, I told *no one* about it at my new job or in my new town. *Literally no one.* To this day, I maintain that this is one of the most important things I've ever not told anyone.

In fact, it wasn't until after I was crying at my desk, alone, after hitting my first best-selling books list, that I went into a trusted coworker's office and told her, "I just hit *USA Today*. I wrote a book, and it hit the best-seller's list."

Needless to say, she was stunned. But even then, I wouldn't tell her my pen name or the title of the book. I'd become a vault, and it changed my life.

## KEEP YOUR DREAMS A SECRET.
## SHOW THE WORLD WHEN THEY COME TRUE.

I truly believe that this is necessary for best-case scenario results. But if it feels right for you to share, do it after your conviction is totally unshakable, and you know it's just a matter of time before your manifestation appears.

### Faking It Until You Make It

To bring whatever it is you want into your life, you have to have the consciousness of it first. To have the consciousness of it, you have to act, think, and feel like you already have what you want. You have to think *from* your new level of consciousness—not *of it*. Again, a subtle difference but a very important one. As mentioned earlier, the easiest way to explain this concept is "faking it until you make it."

It's some of the best advice I've ever gotten. When I was trying to become a full-time author and quit my lawyer job *forever*, I was struggling with the idea of what it meant to be a "real" author, especially when it came to interacting with readers.

I felt like I was trying to be something I wasn't yet. Which is exactly what I was doing—because I hadn't fully acquired the necessary consciousness yet.

At the time, I didn't know anything about consciousness at all; I just felt like I was trying to wear brand-new shoes that were awkward to walk in. A much wiser and more experienced author told me "just fake it until you make it." So, I did. I started to act the way I saw other authors acting, people I respected and whose careers and success I wanted to emulate.

As Jake says, "You can talk about it, or you can be about it."

I stopped dreaming about becoming an author, and I started being one. Instead of feeling like I was an imposter and that I had no right to "pretend" to be an important author when I had only one book published (that totally flopped upon release), I just . . . did it.

It felt like a game of make-believe. I had no idea what I was really doing, but that didn't stop me. In fact, I haven't really known exactly how to do anything I've accomplished—I just did it anyway.

Turns out, not knowing how to do something won't stop you from doing it if you just *try*.

### Using Your Imagination

God gave each of us an imagination for a reason, and it wasn't to imagine worst-case scenarios and relive arguments in our heads. That's using your imagination destructively. By spending time envisioning and imagining things that you don't want, you're just helping to ensure that you get them.

**THE BEST USE OF YOUR IMAGINATION IS TO IMAGINE AND ENVISION ALL THE THINGS *YOU DO WANT*.**

As discussed earlier, you can't get what you want until you know what it is. This is why. You can't imagine yourself into your awesome future unless you know what you want that awesome future to look like.

If you haven't already, take some time to figure it out. Don't worry if it takes you a while to nail down the picture of what you want exactly. Take your time. This is *your life* you're building. Do it with care and intention. And you don't have to know *everything*, you really just need an idea or feeling that represents the essence of what you want.

Again, the Divine Plan includes such incredible things for you that you probably *can't* imagine them right now because they're outside of what you believe is even possible for you. But *anything* is possible. In fact, anything you can imagine or conceive in your mind, no matter how outlandish, seemingly insane, or impossible, is actually totally possible. It wouldn't be possible for you to even imagine it if it wasn't.

Plus, when you're not telling the entire world about your wild and crazy dreams, you don't have to make them realistic because you don't have to justify them to anyone. Let your imagination run wild. Build castles in the sky.

## REMEMBER: UNSELFISH AND CONSTRUCTIVE DESIRES ARE KEY.

The motivation and intention behind what you want matters. They are energy too. Check in with yourself and be honest—are these desires heart-centered and motivated by love, or are they more ego-driven? Ego-driven desires will not produce the same results as those that genuinely come from your heart.

Once you know what you want, how do you do this imagination stuff for best results? Before we knew each other, Jake and I both spent hours each day thinking about and imagining what we wanted. If you don't have that kind of free mental space in your life, do it at night, as you're falling asleep.

## AS YOU'RE FALLING ASLEEP IS THE MOST POWERFUL TIME TO USE YOUR IMAGINATION.

Why? Because you're impressing this picture into your subconscious—into the very fabric of the Universe—as you drift off into dreamland. For the next however many hours you sleep, you're releasing your attachment to it. You're "letting go and letting God." Because while you're asleep, you can't doubt or worry or wonder if or when it's really going to happen.

Doing this takes control. You have to be able to focus your attention on your mental picture of what you want. And not only do you need to focus your attention on it, you need to draw on all the amazing feelings you're going to feel when it comes true.

Neville Goddard calls this the assumption of the wish fulfilled, and it's an essential piece of imagining your way into a life you love.[2]

This is how it works in a nutshell:

If I want to become a tugboat captain, I'm going to fall asleep with a picture in my mind's eye of standing at the helm of my tugboat, feeling the wheel in my hands, my body slightly bouncing as the bow breaks through the chop on the lake as I make my way toward whatever I'm about to use my tugboat to do—as its captain.

But not only am I going to picture doing the things I would do as a tugboat captain, I'm going to hold in my heart the feeling of excitement of doing what I love. I'm going to call up the feelings of gratitude and joy as I get to live this life of my dreams. I'm going to feel the warmth in my chest as I see it all happening in my mind's eye and feel the chill in the air from the wind whipping off the lake. And then I'm going to fall asleep feeling like my dream is already real.

I'm going to do this as often as it feels good. During the day, I'm going to walk around with a smile on my face and excitement in my heart about what's coming because I already know it's as good as done.

The Universe knows exactly what I want. I'm thrilled it has already happened on the invisible planes of my imagination. I know that me envisioning my constructive, unselfish dream is God seeing the Divine Plan unfolding.

I never let any doubt into my mind about whether it's coming true, because it already is true in my mind. I've adopted the belief as part of my consciousness—the only real cause of anything in my life. I know that the outside world just has to catch up with my dream, and it's only a matter of time.

The outside world might see me as what I appear to be now, but in my heart, I'm already a tugboat captain, just waiting for my ship to come in. And I know it will, because I have complete faith, and no doubt and no fear.

That's it. That's the mental part of the creative process.

Imagination plus faith and "faking it until you make it" can change your life radically.

After all, your body doesn't know the difference between something that's really happening and something that's only happening in your imagination. Just like when you watch a scary movie, your heart races, even though you're not being chased by an axe murderer.

As I'm imagining the chop of the waves and the helm in my hand with joy flowing through me because I'm out on the water, living the life of my dreams, my body doesn't know that it's not really happening. My body believes I'm already a tugboat captain, which means I'm acquiring the consciousness of being a tugboat captain.

If I can persist in the consciousness of being a tugboat captain despite going to work at my regular job, the powers of the Universe are going to rearrange things in my life and bring me ideas and opportunities that I can take advantage of that will result in my dream—or something even more perfect for me—becoming my reality.

The question then becomes: if it's this easy to imagine what you want, then why does it seem so hard to see the process through sometimes?

An unavoidable truth is that we are each capable of being our own worst enemy. We might know intellectually that this process works—which it does—but it's those waking hours where problems tend to arise.

It's the thinking about why it hasn't happened yet or how long it's going to take. Or the doubt that creeps in, making us wonder if it's even really possible, and if we're stupid for believing something like this could happen for us. Or it's seeing someone else get that thing we want so badly, and wondering why it didn't come to us first.

All of those things are focusing on the *lack* of what we want, and when we're focusing on *not having it*, the Universe is getting mixed signals from us. It's not sure if we want it anymore because we're spending a lot of energy on noticing we don't have it yet.

The challenge is *knowing*, expecting, having faith, being patient, and listening to the intuitive nudges to take aligned and inspired action to bring the manifestation of the dream into reality.

Also, when someone else gets what you want, you should be *ecstatic*. Why? Because it's proof that it's possible for it to happen. What's more, seeing someone else getting what you want is a common sign that your manifestation is *almost here*. But what do most people do instead when they see someone else getting what they want before they get it? Feel jealous, envious, or outraged that it didn't happen for them first. Those are all surefire ways to negate all the work you've done in envisioning your awesome future. It makes it more likely that you're pushing away the good that was coming straight for you.

The next time you see someone getting what you want, *celebrate for them.* Be excited! Be grateful that it's possible. Cheer for them. Because what you're actually doing is cheering for yourself. Being grateful it's coming to you too. Celebrating that *you're* getting what you want. This is a great way to help your process of manifestation come into form more quickly. Good-feeling emotions are *key* to the entire manifestation process.

## The How and When Isn't Up to You

This can be one of the hardest lessons to learn. The how

something is going to happen and the timetable involved in it coming into manifestation *is not up to you.*

Your job is to:

(1) figure out what you want,

(2) imagine and envision it so God knows that's what you want—or something better,

(3) listen to your intuitive nudges to take fearless, aligned, and inspired action at the appropriate time,

(4) have faith and be patient and poised.

Always remember to leave space for the Universe to knock your socks off and wow you with Its even better plan for you than you had for yourself.

When you start trying to envision *exactly how* this thing that you want is going to come into your life, you're putting limits on Infinite Intelligence, and that's the opposite of what you want to do.

God has ways of accomplishing things we can't begin to fathom. Your manifestation can come into fruition in myriad different ways that you never expect. And what's more, if you can persist in holding the consciousness of what you want for long enough to allow the Universe to move the Divine pieces around to give it to you, it may come in a way that you don't expect at all.

Allow yourself to be amazed, surprised, and delighted by the unconventional, mysterious, and wonderful workings of Infinite Intelligence. Let go of the need to control everything, and let magic unfold in your life in ways that you can't even comprehend right now.

That's the beauty of "letting go and letting God." You don't have to control anything. You don't have to know how it's going to happen.

I *never* know how my dreams are going to come true. But they do. All the time. And it's never how or when I expect. It's always so much better.

Divine Timing is real. We have experienced the perfection of Divine Timing so many times in our lives that there is no doubt that it's way better than anything we could come up with on our own.

The craziest incidence of Divine Timing Jake has ever experienced was arriving into Joplin, Missouri, only twenty minutes before the F5 tornado that destroyed a mile-wide stretch through town. It hit both his rental house and his parents' house, which were located directly across the street from each other.

Jake had been working on the road for months, installing satellite TV, when he got the un-ignorable intuitive message to go home. Immediately. Being no stranger to following his intuition, Jake kicked the rest of his jobs for the day and started the five-hour drive home. He arrived in Joplin with just minutes to spare before the tornado sirens went off.

You might be thinking that this was an instance of crappy Divine Timing, but nothing could be further from the truth. It was perfect.

There was *nowhere* else Jake would have rather been while that tornado hit his parents' house than as close to them as possible, so he could check on them immediately after the destruction was complete.

Plus, God knew Jake needed to be in that bathroom, using his strength to hold that door shut, so he could help protect four other people, including two children. And Jake had to be there, in that moment, to experience the all-important realization that changed who he was and set him on a totally different life path than the one he'd been on when he drove into town twenty minutes earlier.

Divine Timing is real, and it's always working in your favor, even if it doesn't at first appear like it.

When I wanted to quit my legal job forever, I didn't know how long it would take to build an author career that could support me so I wouldn't have to live in my mom's basement. After my second book flopped, I remember sitting on my couch and making this decision: "I don't care if it takes five years. I'm not going to quit trying until it happens."

I told myself that every book that flopped was just money in the bank waiting for when my career finally took off, because I knew readers would fall in love with my breakout book and then go back and read everything I'd ever written. Because that's what my kind of readers did. I believed this because that's what *I did* as a reader.

Divine Timing didn't take five years. From the day I made that vitally important decision of total commitment to my dream, it took five months for it to come true. My third book took off like a rocket ship to the moon, quickly selling a hundred thousand copies, allowing me to save double my annual income from being a lawyer —in only a few months—from doing something I loved.

Eighteen months after I published my first book, with two flops, I quit my job and never negotiated another indemnity clause again.

This really happened. This stuff works. And I didn't even know at the time what I was doing.

Neither did Jake when he was envisioning himself as a superhero action figure every night as he fell asleep. We just . . . did it. It took years before we did the research and made the connections to understand why what we did worked.

We didn't know anything about manifestation. We each just wanted a different life and future for ourselves.

You can do it too. It's not hard. It just takes believing that it works, believing in yourself, assuming the consciousness of who you desire to become, and persisting in that state of consciousness until your outside world catches up to match the new inner you.

**The Infinite Now**

When you're imagining your dreams coming true, don't imagine them as coming true in the far-off future. If you do that, you're always going to be trying to catch up to them.

As we stated earlier, you're living in the infinite now-moment and time isn't real. Which means that you must always envision your dreams coming true and you becoming the person you want to be—*now*. Not years down the road when you think it might be possible. *Now.* This is very important.

If you're constantly envisioning these scenes a year from now, you may never catch up with them. Dream of it happening *now*. Start "faking it until you make it" *now*. Start thinking, speaking, and acting *now* like the person you want to become—the person who *currently has what you want*. The person you're growing into being. The person whose current reality is your dream.

You're sending an incredibly important message to the Universe with your every thought, word, action, reaction, belief, and decision. Make it the right message. Start being like the person you want to become.

**ABOVE ALL, YOU MUST ABSOLUTELY BELIEVE THAT WHATEVER YOU DESIRE IS POSSIBLE *FOR YOU*.**

If you're harboring even a shred of doubt about whether this can actually happen for you, you may be blocking your dream completely. The Universe reads your doubts and also believes it's not possible for you because the Universe is constantly delivering to you what you *believe*. If you can "become as little children"[3] and believe anything is possible, and that you are limitless and the possibilities for your life and future are limitless, then they are. It all comes down to what you believe is possible for *you*.

We told you that you were the key to everything, and you are. How you feel about what you're trying to bring into manifestation and why you're trying to do it will determine whether or not, and how quickly, it happens.

CHOOSE WISELY.
SHUT OUT YOUR FEAR AND DOUBTS.
BELIEVE IT'S POSSIBLE *FOR YOU*.
BELIEVE YOU CAN LIVE THE LIFE OF YOUR DREAMS AND BECOME THE PERSON YOU'VE ALWAYS WANTED TO BE.
THEN PREPARE FOR THE UNIVERSE TO SHOW YOU THE PATH AND FOR MAGIC TO UNFOLD IN YOUR LIFE.

# NINE
## CHANGE YOUR HABITS, CHANGE YOUR LIFE

> Your beliefs become your thoughts.
> Your thoughts become your words.
> Your words become your actions.
> Your actions become your habits.
> Your habits become your values.
> Your values become your destiny.
> – Gandhi

We've talked about your beliefs, your thoughts, your words, and your actions, but Gandhi reminds us that if you want to change your life, you also have to change your habits.

If you want exceptional guidance on how to change and build new habits, James Clear's *Atomic Habits* is a fabulous read and wonderful in audio.

Here are some habits that we quit, and some that we've added to our repertoire or doubled-down on, that have led to our lives becoming immeasurably better.

### Worrying

We quit worrying.

I didn't know you could actually *quit* worrying. Honestly, I didn't even know it was an option until I read *Homeless to Billionaire* when Jake suggested we hit a bookstore in LAX while we were waiting to board a flight to Fiji.[1]

It had never occurred to me that whether I worried about things or not was something I actually had a choice about. I thought people just worried because that's what you do. I thought it was normal to worry. Something you basically *had* to do if you wanted life to turn out the way you wanted.

Turns out, I was massively wrong. Remember, just because something is common doesn't make it normal. Worrying is one of those things.

Worrying is placing your attention on everything you don't want, feeding it all of that precious energy, and helping to ensure what you're worrying about happens in your life instead of things you *actually* want to have happen in your life.

Worrying is doubling down on what you don't want. Worrying is *fear*. Fear is not your friend. We choose faith over fear.

Quitting worrying wasn't the easiest thing I've ever done, but it seemed like the most logical thing to do once I realized the impact of worry. I can't claim that I never have a worrisome thought slip into my mind anymore, but when I do, I toss it on the Holy Fire within and let it burn away.

**SURRENDER IS A FABULOUS WAY TO OVERCOME WORRYING.**

It wasn't until later that I learned that Jake *does not worry about things*. I had no idea that he already knew intuitively what I had to learn from a book. That happens a lot with us.

The good news is, you can quit worrying and focus all that energy on thinking about things *you do want* in your life. We promise it's a much better use of your energy and attention. Plus, you just feel better when you trust that the Universe has your back,

Source is providing everything you need, and Infinite Intelligence is leading you to the path of your highest fulfillment.

Faith is the cure.

**Fear**

We quit fear. Fear isn't real. Babies are only born with two fears—the fear of falling and the fear of loud noises.[2] Those fears keep them alive. But your fears aren't generally keeping you alive. They're keeping you from living your best life.

## QUITTING FEAR IS ALL ABOUT DOUBLING DOWN ON FAITH.

As we said earlier, fear is faith inverted. To quit fear—just like quitting worrying—you have to lean into faith. You also have to trust that there is an unconditionally loving Divine Plan for your life and that it's unfolding perfectly to give you the most soul growth possible in this lifetime that you'll allow.

Fear is what's holding you back from that soul growth. It doesn't matter what the fear is, you don't have to give it your attention or your energy.

The simplest way for handling fear we've ever read came from Emmet Fox, a New Thought and spiritual leader from the early 1900s. When you start thinking about anything you're afraid of, stop thinking about it and start thinking about God instead.[3]

If you're still dealing with societal conditioning around the word God, then think about the Infinite. The Divine. All That Is. The Universe. Love. The word does not matter. What matters is that you take your mind off fear and put it on something so much bigger than you—or any fear.

Plus, fearing something just ensures that you're magnetically attracting that exact thing into your reality even faster.

## FEAR IS A POWERFUL, EXTREMELY LOW-VIBRATION EMOTION.

Decisions made from a place of fear will never be as good as decisions made from a place of love. Why? Because if you're feeling the emotion of fear, you're at the bottom of the emotional frequency guidance scale created by Esther and Jerry Hicks and their guide, Abraham, which we first learned about in Gabrielle Bernstein's book, *Super Attractor*. [4] Also at the bottom of this extremely useful scale are emotions like powerlessness, despair, depression, and grief.[5]

When you're living in this low vibration, you can't see all the amazing options that are available to you because you've tuned into a very heavy, dense frequency where creative, inspired solutions usually aren't present. And as you probably already guessed, when you're feeling fear, the Universe knows that, and in response, sends you more situations, people, and experiences to be fearful of. Much of society is engaged in this fear-based living, but you don't have to live that way.

## YOU'RE ALLOWED TO BE A CREATIVE REBEL, AND CHOOSE LOVE, TRUST, AND FAITH OVER FEAR.

It's a massive shift in the way that you think, speak, believe, act, react, and live. When you trade in fear for faith, you become more powerful, more loving, more peaceful, more joyful, and generally have more enjoyable life experiences.

Florence gives advice about dispelling fear in *The Game of Life and How to Play It*. She says that you must face the lion of your fear by simply walking up to it.[6] Florence maintains that your fear will disappear when you're brave enough to walk up to it and face it. "Courage contains genius and magic," says Florence.[7]

She offers the example of a friend who was afraid to walk under ladders due to superstition. The woman couldn't go somewhere she needed to go because there was a ladder in the way. When Florence got her pumped up to face her fear and walk up to that lion of a ladder, it had disappeared. Florence wasn't surprised at all! [8]

How many times have you had to face the scary thing you feared and then learned it wasn't nearly as terrifying as you'd built it up to be in your head? Or how many times did you end up not having to face the thing at all once you built up the courage to do it? We have experienced this personally many, many times.

## FEAR IS NOT REAL.
## FEAR IS A LIE AND AN ILLUSION STANDING
## BETWEEN YOU AND THE LIFE OF YOUR DREAMS.
## DON'T LET IT. HAVE FAITH, NOT FEAR.

**Stress**

Stress can kill you. I'm not joking. It almost killed me.

"Stress is responsible for up to 90 percent of all doctor office visits," according to Dr. Herbert Benson of Harvard Medical School.[9] Dr. Bruce Lipton, a pioneer stem-cell biologist, had a fabulous discussion of stress and its effects in one of my very favorite books, *The Biology of Belief*, which I think everyone should read. Stress leads to all sorts of negative health outcomes, including cancer and autoimmune diseases.

Quitting stress is one of the best decisions we've ever made in our lives. But how do you do it?

Decide that you're not going to let stress rule your life anymore. Slow down. Simplify your life and everything in it. Stop getting involved in drama and other people's lives—it's none of your business anyway. Start practicing mindfulness and put your health nearer the top of your priority list.

## YOU ARE IN CONTROL OF YOUR STRESS LEVEL.

It's not a good thing to be under stress. It doesn't make you more important or more successful, regardless of what you've been shown, modeled, or programmed with.

I grew up professionally in an environment where people wore stress as a badge of honor. It's not. It's one of the best ways to destroy your health and ultimately your life.

Publishing deadlines for books ran our life for years. Everything rose and fell based on how the book was going. I was a stressed-out disaster of a mess—and Jake felt every single bit of it too. We were making millions, but it didn't always feel worth it because of the stress I had put us under. It destroyed my health and made me think I was dying of a heart attack—instead of experiencing a massive, gnarly panic attack that ended with a bunch of paramedics in our kitchen at midnight. That was my wakeup call that I had to change and stress had to go.

Here's the good news:

**YOU CAN TOTALLY COME BACK FROM STRESS.**

Your body can heal. You can be happy and joyful and live a stress-free life. However, in order to do this, you have to change and you have to change your lifestyle. We did, and it was so worth it.

We have found that the easiest way to eliminate stress from our life is to double down on faith and trust in the Divine Plan and Divine Timing. We know that everything is always working out in our best interest, even if it doesn't look like it. We also know that time is only a construct of man and is elastic.

I don't worry about having enough time to get things done anymore, because I know that what is meant to get done will get done. If I can't get it all done without stressing myself to the max, then it's not meant to get done.

Source doesn't expect you to run yourself ragged every hour of every day. Source will never ask you to do more in the Divine Plan than you are capable of doing in a healthy, life-affirming manner.

It's the human part of us, rather than the Divine, that thinks we need to control every little thing so that life works out the way we want. It turns out, life works out way better when you flow with it rather than white-knuckling your way through it or trying to wrestle it into submission.

### HAVE FAITH. LEARN TO FLOW.

Learn to be okay with things not working out exactly the way you want them to. They're not always supposed to. Leave room for the magic of the Universe in your life rather than filling it with stress.

It took me years to learn this lesson, but I couldn't deny it was a better way to live when I saw it play out so perfectly in my life so many times.

Every time I was on a tight deadline for a book, I'd wake up to a day where I just *did not feel like writing at all*. Like, *not happening today, no way*. In my earlier years, I would beat myself up constantly for that entire day because I wasn't writing when I thought that I should have been because the hours to my deadline were ticking down.

So, instead of just enjoying the day off that I clearly needed at the time, I would feel guilty and crappy and I was not pleasant to be around. Then out of nowhere, an idea would pop into my head with the perfect scene or twist or thing that I needed to make the book *way* better. Always. Like clockwork.

When that happens to you enough times, you start to realize there's a bigger plan in play that transcends your idea of how things are supposed to be going. That's the Divine Plan. When I finally realized I could give myself grace and take the day off and let the Universe tell me what I was missing from my book, I became a much happier writer.

You will never stress yourself into good situations without major costs to your health. It's just not worth it. Now I flow—which it turns out Jake has been doing *all along*. *Naturally*. Because that's just how he is.

He helped me realize that life is much better when you allow the current to take you where you need to go rather than fighting against it and believing you need to swim upstream all the time to get what you want, which was what I'd been trained to do.

Now, anytime I start to feel stress creeping up, I immediately look at my life to pinpoint the source. Is it the new deadline I set? Okay, noted. Then I accept the fact that the timing for the project isn't necessarily in my control because Divine Timing knows better than me. I also know, at a soul-deep level, that everything's going to work out perfectly, exactly the way Source intends, even if it doesn't match the picture in my head that I had for success.

Letting go and letting God is the greatest tool for kicking stress we've ever found. Plus, the more faith you have, the easier it gets to live like this. It might take practice at first, but eventually it becomes second nature, just like getting all stressed out over everything used to be. Putting your energy into faith invites miraculous Divine solutions into your life, which is way better.

**Consuming Negative Content**

We quit consuming negative content of any kind.

I once heard Dr. Joe Dispenza say something in a video about not consuming any content that you don't want to have happen to you, and it rocked me. But our lives have changed dramatically for the better by listening to his advice.

> **YOUR SUBCONSCIOUS IS TAKING IN EVERY BIT OF THE CONTENT YOU CONSUME, RIGHT ALONG WITH YOU, AND IT'S FROM YOUR SUBCONSCIOUS THAT THE VERY CREATIVE POWERS OF THE UNIVERSE GO TO WORK.**

If you're constantly watching horror movies, don't be surprised if you attract some scary experiences into your life. The same goes with watching news channels that pump out fear, anger, blame, judgment, negativity, and hate—for anyone or anything. Focusing your attention on negative content isn't doing you any favors.

Remember: beautiful mind, beautiful life. It's more challenging to have a beautiful life when you're filling your mind full of terrifying stuff, someone's judgmental or hateful opinion, or pointless crap. Fill your subconscious with good stuff instead for the Universe to work with to create your awesome future.

**BE INTENTIONAL ABOUT WHAT YOU CONSUME, ESPECIALLY YOUR CONTENT.**

We consume content that leaves us feeling uplifted, like anything is possible and that we can achieve our dreams and have the life that we love. Fill your life with inputs that make you feel awesome and empower you. Be ruthless about weeding out content that leaves you feeling disempowered, fearful, angry, enraged, judgmental, frustrated, hopeless, or lost. You don't need that in your life. It's not helping you create anything good.

Plus, whenever you're watching or consuming entertainment or media, be aware that you are being programmed. It's literally called *television programming.* It's not always intentional by the creator, either. Often, the creator is simply conditioned and programmed too and through the creation of their content, they're simply perpetuating that programming and conditioning.

I know this for a fact because I've done it.

We don't drink alcohol at all anymore, but when I look back at the books I wrote—which often featured alcohol as being an appropriate way to deal with life and its challenges—I see the societal programming that I have since thrown off. There's a reason I don't write things like I used to anymore. I know more now than I knew then, but I've forgiven myself for any negative or programmed aspect of anything I created in the past. I could only create from my then-current level of consciousness. You can't fault anyone for that, including yourself. All you can do is learn, grow, evolve, and become a better version of yourself every day.

One way to ensure you're doing that is taking a hard look at the content you consume and being mindful and aware when you're choosing it. A beautiful mind really does lead to a beautiful life.

## Social Media Addiction

We quit scrolling through social media, and then stopped spending any of our free time on social media at all.

While technology can be used for wonderful connective purposes, and we use it for our businesses, it seems like social media has become, for many people, one big toxic judgment zone. It's easy to get suckered into being emotionally hooked into post after post.

When you get emotionally hooked by something you see on social media, you're feeding it your energy because you're giving it your incredibly valuable attention. Every time you engage with social media, feeling judgmental, outraged, disgusted, angry, frustrated, or any other negative emotion, imagine little cords of your energy attaching to the content and draining right out of you.

This is your vital life energy you're giving away, out of the *only moment* you have any power to change your life.

Just because it's socially acceptable to spend hours a day getting riled up over things you see on the internet, it's not beneficial for you. And it's certainly not helping you direct your attention and energy toward building your awesome future.

Be aware, this is definitely an addiction. Apps are specifically designed to addict you and keep you in the app and coming back for more.

Have you noticed that your body is connected to this addiction as well?

How many times a day do you reach for your phone? Does your thumb know exactly where to tap that little app icon to bring up your social media world? Do you get sucked in and feel like you can't quit, even though you *know* you have other things you could or should be doing?

It's okay. Tech geniuses built social media platforms deliberately to affect you this way. Like any addiction, you can quit. It just takes wanting to do it and substituting the habit with a new one, like replacing reaching for your phone with reaching for a great book instead.

Spending hours per day on social media—like I used to—left me feeling drained, stressed to the max, in a judgment coma, and gossiping about people I didn't even know in real life.

All of those things were dragging my vibration down and ensuring that my life experience wasn't what I wanted it to be. The addiction also interfered with me creating the things my heart and soul were crying out for me to create.

Now I spend no more than an average of one hour or less per day touching my phone. Because of this choice, I'm happier, healthier, more vibrant, more successful, more creative, more loving, and more in love with life than ever before.

**DON'T LET SOCIAL MEDIA STEAL YOUR AWESOME FUTURE. IT'S NOT WORTH IT.**

If you need to use social media, use it as a tool. It can be very useful for business, but as Jake has always told me repeatedly, "likes don't pay the bills."

Don't get sucked in. And be honest with yourself about whether you're addicted. Jake and I both were, but it's okay. You don't have to stay that way. We didn't.

### Living Your Life to Please Others

We quit living our lives to please or placate others.

You have a unique life path. Every single one of us does, and it's unbelievably perfect for each of us. Living your life to please or placate other people most likely means you're missing out on at least some of the awesomeness of your unique life path.

We understand—going your own way isn't always the easiest thing to do, especially when others would prefer you to take another route or give you well-meaning advice. Considering and weighing wisdom when it's offered is wise. You can learn so much from other people who have had experiences beyond yours.

However, no one else knows exactly what is right for you but *you*. No one else has your heart, which is your personalized guidance system for this life. No one but you can listen to your heart as it leads you along your unique journey through life.

**IT'S A BOLD, COURAGEOUS MOVE TO LIVE AS YOUR TRUE, AUTHENTIC SELF AND WALK YOUR OWN LIFE PATH.**

That's at the heart of being a creative rebel: being brave enough to be yourself. All of yourself. Regardless of whether anyone else approves of you or likes you. It's the ultimate act of rebellion to be true to your heart and live your truth out in the open, fearlessly loving and accepting all parts of yourself, exactly as Spirit created you.

When you live from your heart as opposed to living according to the desires and dictates of others and society, your life changes. Often radically and for your own best interest.

Are you brave enough to be yourself and live the uniquely awesome life path that Infinite Intelligence has specially earmarked just for you?

If you're not already, you can absolutely become that person. Have no fear, Spirit never gives up on *anyone*. Ever.

You can decide at any moment that you're going to throw off the fear of being different and live from your heart. And if you want to win this game of life yourself, it's 100 percent necessary.

You're never going to reach your highest and most fulfilling Divine Destiny and become the person you came here to be if you're constantly worrying about what others think or living your life to please them.

This is your life. Your one incarnation in this body.

You have a limited amount of time to become the person you came here to be and do the things you came here to do. Don't waste it trying to please everyone else but yourself.

## YOU MATTER.
## YOUR LIFE MATTERS.
## WHAT YOU DO WITH IT MATTERS.

Why not make it something that's uniquely awesome and perfect for you?

### The Magic of Meditation

Meditation is a game changer. There's no other way to put it. After three years of trying one method after another, it finally "clicked" for me, and it felt like a whole new world I didn't know existed before opened up in my life. A world where there are *no limits* and anything is possible.

Meditation is *amazing*.

It's so much more than just sitting in silence, trying not to think, like we originally thought.

It's also not a chore. Meditation is a *gift*.

Although this is a topic that deserves its own book, here are the basics:

Meditation has massive physical, mental, emotional, and spiritual benefits that are really only experienced when you commit to a regular, consistent meditation practice.

How do you do that? Decide you're going to have a meditation practice and start meditating every single day.

How do you actually meditate?

There are a million and one ways to meditate. There are tons of different methods that have been developed by all sorts of different people.

Many people describe meditation as sitting with your eyes closed, focused on your breathing rather than your thoughts. Some apps have you count your breaths or imagine filling your body with light. Still others play tones that you get lost in or match your breathing to. Then there's meditation focused on mantra where you transcend from the level of individual mind to the quantum. There are *so many* different meditation methods. Plus, there are thousands of guided meditations offered by many kinds of people for all sorts of different purposes.

There are *so many* different options you can choose from when it comes to meditating. The most important thing is that you find something that works *for you*. That may not be the same thing that works for us or for anyone else.

After years of attempting to cultivate an effective meditation practice for myself, I realized no two people will ever have the exact same meditation practices. It's impossible. Meditation is totally unique to every individual because we're all unique.

However, after three years of trying many different options and feeling like a less than master meditator, I finally came to a few realizations that helped me make the leap from sitting there with my eyes closed, pushing my thoughts away and focusing on my breathing, to actually communing with the Divine easily, regularly, and with great joy and bliss.

Why and how did my meditations change, you might ask? What was the secret information I discovered that helped me to make this massive leap?

*Purpose.*

Everything is different when you do it with purpose.

I realized through meditation I could access my subconscious mind and rewrite the faulty programs that had been installed there so I could produce instead more love, happiness, joy, health, abundance, success, prosperity, peace, and compassion in my life. That's when I really got serious about it. Dr. Joseph Murphy and others refer to this type of meditation as scientific prayer.[10]

I quit sitting in silence feeling like I was wasting my time and started instead focusing on letting go and not trying so hard.

With meditation, there actually *is* a sort of goal—to allow your brain wave state to shift. I feel this shift as my body becomes more rigid and my skin seems to buzz with energy (similar to a body buzz from cannabis). When I experience that *feeling,* I know I'm there. The place I want to be.

Once you're in this state, you can rewrite your subconscious programming, talk to your higher self and spiritual guides, ask questions and receive answers, envision or experience beautiful scenes from your future, meet with angels and other energetic beings who love you unconditionally, commune with Jesus on the top of a mountain, visit temples or ancient libraries in the sky, recharge your spiritual batteries, or sink into nothingness within the blackness and experience for yourself the true nature of the Divine.

It's magical.

There's no limit to what you can do in meditation. *None.* It's an unlimited world you can access for guidance, peace, healing, love, to create your future, to release your past, forgive yourself and others, personally know God, and so much more.

There's a description of the virtual reality world, the OASIS, in the beginning of the film adaptation of Ernest Cline's *Ready Player One* that instantly brought to my mind the magic of meditation:

It's a place where the limits of reality are your own imagination. You can do anything, go anywhere.

Like the vacation planet. Surf a fifty-foot wave in Hawaii. You can ski down the pyramids. You can climb Mt. Everest . . . with Batman.

People come to the OASIS for all the things they can do, they stay because of all the things they can be.[11]

The only difference with meditation is that it's free, you can start right now, it doesn't require virtual reality, and you don't need fancy haptic gloves or a boot suit.

Meditation truly is magical. It can be done in many different ways—sitting in silence, walking, dancing, hiking, or whatever. A full discussion is beyond the purview of this book, but we suggest you investigate any methods of meditation that seem to call to you, if or when they call to you.

The health benefits are undeniable. And Jake can attest to just how much purposeful meditation has altered my personality—making me more loving, joyful, compassionate, patient, and *definitely* way more peaceful. I can attest to the very same about him after he started too.

Meditation absolutely has the power to change your life and everything in it. The trick is figuring out your practice. If you've been at it for a while and still aren't seeing results, don't give up. Keep trying. Keep learning about meditation and different methods until you find the perfect practice for you. It will happen if you want it to. It took me three years of daily effort, but none of that was wasted. The benefits are cumulative, even if you're not experiencing mystical magic every meditation session.

Here's one really important tip I learned from Dr. Joe Dispenza (who has turned his guided meditations into a science and an art):

**THE BIG CHANGES HAPPEN AFTER YOU GET UP FROM YOUR MEDITATION.**

Whatever change you're trying to make while you're "in there" must be brought through into your reality when you leave your meditation.

For instance, if you're meditating to become a more joyful, loving, compassionate person, then when you get up from meditation, you need to start *being* more joyful, loving, and compassionate in reality, even if you're just faking it until you make it. This is wildly important. You are the one who must start acting like the person you want to become, even if it feels weird at first.

Don't forget this step. It helps ground the energetic changes from your meditation into your world. But when you leave your meditation feeling like you've been plugged into a direct line to the very love and heart of the Universe and your system is thrumming with bliss, it's a lot easier.

You still have to do it, though, even if other people are confused about you suddenly being in a better mood, for seemingly no reason.

## MEDITATION IS MAGICAL.

It can absolutely change your life. When or if you feel so moved to try it (or go back to it), we totally recommend giving it a shot.

### A Positive Mental Attitude

Anyone can be negative. *Anyone*. It's easy, it's cheap, and it takes no effort. Positivity, on the other hand, takes strength. It's not always easy. Sometimes it feels downright near impossible, but then you find *something* to grasp onto as a silver lining in a dark cloud.

Positivity isn't cheap. It's expensive because it takes effort. Not everyone seems to be able to manage a positive attitude, but those who can—and especially those who have cultivated one out of the depths of a formerly negative self—know the truth:

## A positive attitude is one of the most valuable traits a person can possess.

Once upon a time, I had a relentlessly positive attitude. It was literally bred into me by my parents, who both read self-help books like *Success Through a Positive Mental Attitude* and *The Power of Positive Thinking* before I was even born.

I had no idea a positive attitude was such an asset. Everything just seemed to go pretty right in my life, and I achieved every goal I set.

And then one day, I lost the relentless part of my positivity. I let negativity slip inside the gates. The gold that had been groomed into me slipped right out of my hands because I didn't know what I had in my possession before that moment. I didn't realize how valuable a relentlessly positive, can-do attitude was. I literally didn't know there was another way to go through life.

Until I let negativity grow. It was easy. It took nothing to find things to complain about or point out that were going wrong. The longer I did it, the more all-encompassing of a habit it became. Until at one point, positivity was essentially dead in my life. Instead of all the solutions that used to easily come to my mind when faced with an obstacle, I could only tell anyone who would listen about why whatever I was worrying about wasn't going to work or how hard it was or how much stress I was under.

Negativity became part of my story. It became part of my consciousness. And then it became part of who I was, a part that made me miserable and trashed more days of my life and Jake's life than I can count offhand.

But they all led me to a very important moment, the moment I finally realized exactly how valuable a positive attitude was. It's worth a lot more than most people know, because they've never lost one and had to go back on the path to regaining it.

It takes work. It takes effort. It takes changing who you are. It takes changing your story about yourself in your head. It takes changing your consciousness.

It takes deciding that you're not going to take the cheap and easy route anymore, complaining about anything and everything just because you can. It takes deciding that you're not that person anymore. It takes deciding that you're more than equal to handling the challenges that come up along your path, and that you can always find a silver lining because there's always one to be found.

It takes not being scared to be someone new around the people in your life who have grown to expect certain responses from you. It takes strength, and you have that inside you.

If you've fallen into the trap of negativity, it's okay. Negativity has been programmed into you by entertainment, media, and pop culture for *years*. It's been programmed into you by the people around you who were programmed to be negative before you were even born.

But the best part is that you can change the program at any moment. You just have to decide you want to, and then start doing it.

Don't worry about messing up and falling back into your old negative habits. If it happens, no big deal. Catch yourself and go back to being positive. It gets easier in time.

Your life will change. Solutions appear more quickly, more easily, and more creatively. And then eventually, being positive is so ingrained that you don't even think about it anymore. Positivity is part of who you are. It's how you view life. It's part of the story you tell yourself about yourself. It's part of your consciousness. It becomes who you are.

**POSITIVITY IS POWER. NEVER DOUBT IT.**

If you've already got a positive mental attitude, cherish it and be grateful you have an asset worth more than its weight in gold. A positive mental attitude wins the day, every time.

### Tuning in to Your Body

When you're making decisions and considering choices, check in with your body. While your brain can't tell truth from falsehood, your body can give you wonderful clues about whether the decision or choice you're considering is right for you.

When you're thinking about your options, pay attention to

where you feel the response in your body. Do you feel a twisting, sinking, or sick feeling in your gut, or does your entire body seem to go weak when you consider the choice? Those are all great signs that the option you're considering is either not right for you or is outside of your integrity.

Do you feel a warmth in your chest or does your heart feel like it's growing and expanding and leaping with joy when you consider the choice or option? Do you feel stronger, more confident, and full of energy? Those are all great signs that your higher self—the divinity within you—is cheering on the choice or option you're considering.

**LISTEN TO THOSE FEELINGS IN YOUR BODY.**

Get in tune with your body, tap into your intuition and perceive the wisdom of your heart, which is the wisdom of Infinite Intelligence. You are being guided at all times—including when to take breaks and rest—if you can just figure out how to recognize the signs.

Jake and I both learned this lesson ourselves before we met. While he listened to his intuition and his body more consciously, I listened purely on instinct. But we both agree, you only have to ignore a few of those "feelings" in your body and experience the consequences before you really start paying close attention and following the signals.

**YOUR HEART KNOWS THINGS THAT IT HAS NO RATIONAL REASON TO KNOW. YOUR HIGHER SELF HAS A MUCH BROADER PERSPECTIVE THAN THE HUMAN PART OF YOU THAT CAN'T SEE THE WHOLE PICTURE.**

Take advantage of the clues your body offers and really pay attention to how it reacts when you're weighing your options and considering your choices.

A few years ago, I started consciously making all of my decisions like this—using my body's reactions and listening to my heart—and it hasn't led me wrong, even though it has led me down some new pathways leading completely into the unknown.

That's where faith and trust come in. I know the unknown is where magic happens, and I'm totally okay with not knowing until it's time for me to know.

It's a completely different way to live compared to rationalizing everything with your mind and using only data and facts to make decisions.

> **FOLLOWING YOUR HEART, YOUR INTUITION, AND YOUR BODY'S GUIDANCE CAN LEAD TO NEW LEVELS OF INNER PEACE.**

That's what it has done for us. Once you get used to living like this, it actually feels really great.

We don't worry about making the wrong decisions anymore. We just feel our way through and trust that the Universe is leading us to our highest fulfillment and greatest good.

So far, it's pretty magical. And we can honestly say that we would never go back to living the way we used to. This feels much too good and has led to many wonderful outcomes.

### Making the Changes

Becoming who you're meant to be and creating a life you love will always involve change and risk. Trying something new, regardless of how small or innocuous, is what keeps us thriving.

Routine has its time, place, and purpose, but trying something new or having the courage to step outside the box is a gift and a strength that can truly change your life.

You are the captain of your own ship. You decide whether tomorrow is exactly the same as today. You decide whether and when you step onto a better, healthier, happier, more prosperous, more loving or whatever path that you desire for this life journey. You have the keys to this car. Your choices plot the map. Free will is part of the game of life, and you have to act occasionally. This is why you have a body. If life were purely a mental game, you wouldn't need one. But you do because action is required.

You can choose to tread water for the rest of your life and never change, but that's boring and tiring. Plus, stagnation leads to decay, and that's not what you truly want.

To change your consciousness, you have to make new choices and live them out in the world. This means you're probably going to have to try something new. As adults, that can be intimidating, mostly because we're afraid of sucking at things and looking stupid.

**DON'T LET THE FEAR OF LOOKING STUPID STOP YOU FROM TRYING SOMETHING NEW.**

Babies, fawns, and colts all wobble when they stand the first time. Do you think that makes them stupid? No, they're learning to walk. Cut yourself some slack. Remember what it's like to be a kid and mostly suck at everything you try. You weren't stupid then—you were just learning new things. It's okay.

**YOU CAN GIVE YOURSELF PERMISSION TO SUCK.**

I do it every single time I sit down to write something new. It's a magical permission slip that takes all the pressure off and allows me to spread my wings and venture into new territory without being critical of how things appear to be going.

Becoming the best version of yourself and living a life you love is going to involve learning and trying new things. You can do it. Eventually these new things that you're learning and trying will become normal feeling habits, just like the ones you currently have.

Except, these will be habits you deliberately chose so you can begin living the life of your dreams and become the person you want to become. Give it a shot and stick with it. You truly have no idea what amazing outcomes are possible for you or how soon your dreams could start becoming your reality.

With potential rewards so great, trying something new—*being* someone new—and feeling a little awkward or silly while you get used to it doesn't seem like that big of a risk.

Try it.

You never know where it could lead.

# TEN
## HEALTH IS WEALTH

*Investments in yourself and your health will always pay dividends.*
— Jacob Wilson

When Jake and I met, he looked like a god. He had for years before we met, and over six years later, he still does.

The man embodies health to such a degree that just being around him actually makes you healthier. His very consciousness of health —because *he is health*—heals those in his presence and helps them become healthier.

This is no joke. I've experienced it firsthand and watched it affect every open-minded person (and some not so open-minded) with whom Jake has consistent and regular interaction.

The influence of Jake's health consciousness is magical. I call it "the Jake Effect," and it changed my life in the best way possible. The opportunity to assume his consciousness of health after experiencing it on a daily basis is one of the greatest gifts I have ever been given, aside from Jake himself. It's something I value above almost anything else in my life.

Vibrant health is one of those things that you can't truly appreciate until you've experienced it. People might think they know what it's like, but until you've lived several years straight with almost no health problems and wake up feeling good nearly *every single day* without needing medication of any kind, you don't.

**IT'S *WONDERFUL* TO BE HEALTHY. IT MAKES EVERYTHING ELSE IN LIFE INFINITELY BETTER.**

I had no idea life could be this good. But Jake did, because Jake *is* health. He embodies it. He lives it. And it's amazing.

When he told me years ago that he doesn't get sick, I was mind-boggled. I didn't know you could just decide not to get sick or that it was possible not to get sick. I thought everyone got sick on occasion when they came into contact with sick people or germs or whatever.

But that was before I understood what it meant to have the consciousness of health. The most important words Jake ever told me to say to myself—on repeat—were these:

**I AM HEALTHY.**

Remember, whatever you put after "I AM," you are in the process of becoming.

When Jake told me all this stuff in the beginning of our relationship, I didn't believe him. I really didn't. I didn't think it could be that easy.

Jake reminds me that I was so skeptical that I wouldn't even *say* the words "I am healthy" at first. Because in my mind, it wasn't true.

I'd been "sick" since I was three years old, diagnosed with chronic illnesses that I was told could never be cured. Remember what happens when you tell a child under the age of six something? They believe it to be the gospel truth, it downloads directly into their subconscious, and it affects the rest of their life—until the program is changed.

That's what happened to me. I lived like the girl in the bubble who couldn't come into contact with countless things or I'd end up in the emergency room.

I spent thirty-three years of my life going back and forth from one doctor's office to another, and then to the pharmacy, trying to find health through conventional medicine and prescription drugs.

But I never got healthy. Not truly. Not ever.

Not until Jake.

Not until he showed me there was a different way to think and to live.

If you're thinking this sounds crazy, that you can't think your way into good health, then you've never met Jake. And also, you've been programmed to believe what you currently believe, just like I had been.

Many of these programs are not true. I'm proof. My doctors essentially told me all my life that I'd die without taking prescription drugs. False.

At the time of writing this, I haven't taken a prescription drug in nearly two years—and most of them I quit taking over three years ago. Not only have I *not* died, I'm the healthiest and most vibrant I've ever been in my entire life.

I finally know what it's like to be healthy. Truly healthy. Vibrantly healthy. And I'm here to tell you that it's wonderful—and you can do it too.

Our bodies are miraculous self-healing machines that "modern medicine" doesn't understand in its entirety. There have been instant healings of almost every kind of condition and disease in our lifetimes. There are countless stories of people whose cancer just disappears, and there are people who can suddenly walk who couldn't walk before. Even instances of the blind becoming able to see.

The miraculous is possible, every single day—if you believe it is.

I didn't used to believe. But now I do, because I live it.

This is what Jake taught me:

## HEALTH IS A RESULT OF THE DECISIONS YOU MAKE EVERY SINGLE DAY, ALL DAY LONG.

Health actually comes from acts of self-love.

Here are a few basics to get us started:

*You are meant to be healthy.* The Infinite Intelligence that created you intended for you to know vibrant health. It is your birthright and available to everyone, regardless of your age or condition.

*You cannot buy health and no one else can do it for you.* It's not possible. Your health is your responsibility—not your doctor's, your significant other's, your trainer's, or a politician's. Health is a DIY project. You have to do it yourself, for yourself.

*Everything you put in your body and on your body affects your health.* So does your environment and everything in it, including things you can't see.

*Health isn't complicated, and it isn't only for special people.* Health is consciousness, which means it's for *everyone* who acquires the consciousness of health.

### Health Consciousness

How do you get the Jake Effect if you can't live with him like I do? It's actually not that hard. First, you start thinking about it—because that's where everything starts—in your thoughts.

Start asking yourself questions like:

What do healthy people do?<br>
How do they think?<br>
What do they think about?<br>
What do they eat?<br>
How do they speak?<br>
What do they talk about?<br>
How do they spend their time?

**Where do they put their attention?**
**What are they doing and thinking that's different**
**from what you're doing and thinking?**
**Who are they being?**

*Healthy people make health a priority in their lives.* It's a necessary filter through which they run all of their decisions through, every day, all day long.

*Healthy people think about what they're putting in their bodies.* They choose foods that have nutritional value and are good for their health. This doesn't mean they only eat organic lettuce for every meal, but it does mean they make good choices about what they eat the vast majority of the time. Healthy food doesn't have to be complicated, it just needs to be food that nourishes your body appropriately.

*Healthy people live a healthy lifestyle.* They make healthy choices about how they spend their time. They value health. They speak about health and their healthy activities. They talk about how healthy they are and how much they love being healthy. They spend their time doing things that enhance or maintain their health.

### HEALTHY PEOPLE EMBODY HEALTH.

That's literally how it works.

So, how do you go from thinking about health to embodying it? You decide you're going to be healthy. You start faking it until you make it.

And that starts with making different decisions. Think about what you put in your mouth and in your body *before* you put it in your mouth or your body. You know that guilt you feel when you eat an overindulgent meal or dessert or the entire bag of chips or box of cookies? That guilt you're feeling is a message from your higher self that you're making a decision that doesn't align with the person you really want to be.

Deep down, you probably already know if the decisions you're making are good for your health or not. That's why you feel guilty when you make decisions that aren't healthy. Your higher self *wants* you to be healthy. You're so much more useful in the Divine Plan when you're physically, mentally, emotionally, and spiritually healthy and capable.

Your body is your one vehicle for this lifetime. It's your temple where the power of Infinite Intelligence is flowing through you. Treat it with love. Feed it nourishing foods that provide all the appropriate things it needs to thrive—a healthy balance of nutrient-dense protein, healthy fats, and clean carbs. And before you ask what that balance is, know that it's different for everybody.

What works for us may not work for you. Learning about your particular body and what it needs is so important. Just because a lot of people are losing weight by eating a particular diet doesn't mean it's the right thing for you and your body. Food-sensitivity and gut-health tests are powerful and can provide you with valuable knowledge about what your body needs, doesn't like, and shouldn't have.

This is where people often emotionalize things—when they fear they're going to have to give up something that they enjoy.

We can tell you with 100 percent certainty that *nothing* tastes as good as being healthy feels. *Literally nothing.*

I never thought I'd ever be able to go a single day without chocolate. You could never have convinced me that anything would be worth giving up chocolate (and we're not saying you have to give up chocolate in order to be vibrantly healthy). But when I discovered that my body does not tolerate any dairy products at all without me paying a price for it, it eventually just wasn't worth it anymore. I value how I feel so much more than how chocolate tastes.

Now I don't care at all that I don't eat chocolate. I don't miss it either. I'm too busy feeling amazing every day and living the life of my dreams. What is chocolate compared to that? Nothing. It's absolutely *nothing.*

This may not be convincing to you yet, but when you start walking the road to health with intention, you'll realize that many of the things you've always eaten and loved just aren't worth it anymore because the food you eat affects how you feel—physically, mentally, and emotionally. You'll realize that you don't want to give up feeling amazing for anything. It's just too good to let go of.

I didn't understand before how Jake could take one bite of some incredible dessert and then push it away, while I was in the process of hoovering down an entire plateful. He knew after tasting the super-sugary sweetness that it was going to make him feel like crap, and it wasn't worth it to him.

I, on the other hand, didn't know anything other than generally always feeling like crap at that point, so I kept eating.

## ONCE YOU START EATING TO FEEL GOOD, EVERYTHING CHANGES.

You start making the connection between what you put in your body and how it makes you feel, which is a major milestone. It doesn't matter if you still eat food that makes you feel like crap on occasion as long as you can recognize and understand the effects it's going to have on you *before* you eat it. Then you make informed choices.

Don't bury your head in the sand and pretend you can eat crappy fast food and junk every day and live the life of your dreams with vibrant health. A steady diet of junk food and vibrant health are mutually exclusive, no matter how badly you don't want that to be true.

Listen to your body. Pay attention to how you feel after you eat. If you feel bad after eating certain foods, don't eat them anymore. Wild animals wouldn't.

Popping heartburn relief medication or dairy pills just so you can eat certain types of foods and not experience the bad feelings doesn't make it better. You don't know what else that pill is doing to your body or to your microbiome.

**The Easiest Way to Live and Eat Healthy**

The easiest way to live and eat healthy is to find a diet and workout plan that makes you feel good. When I quit eating and working out to lose weight and instead started eating and moving my body for the sole purpose of *feeling good*, everything changed.

Losing weight became a distant secondary goal to restoring my mental health—which only happens when you restore your *health*. It's no coincidence that there are massive mental health problems in America when you take a look at the standard American diet and lifestyle. It's not designed to produce happy, healthy, vibrant people. It's designed to produce exactly what it produces—overweight, chronically ill, unhappy people.

We all know that it's healthier to eat real food like vegetables, fruits, lean protein, and whole food carbs than it is to eat junk food and fast food. So, why don't we? Lots of reasons. The one I hear most often is, "I don't have time."

What is more important to spend your time on than making sure your body keeps functioning, so you stay happy and healthy and can live an awesome life? Wealth is not more important than your health. In fact, if you want to enjoy your wealth, you're going to want great health. You can't buy that, no matter how much money you make.

Another huge reason people don't eat healthy is the billions of dollars spent on marketing by companies who hire people who know *exactly* how your body and mind work. Those advertisements that leave your mouth watering for whatever you saw on a screen have been created by people who know that your body doesn't have to smell or see the real thing in order to make your mouth water.[1] They get paid the big bucks because they know how to hook you into wanting what they're selling. It's literally their job to make you crave crap that's bad for you. Avoid the advertisements, and they don't work for long.

There aren't many flashy marketing campaigns for healthy food because it's mostly sold by farmers, not international conglomerates with shareholders, quarterly earnings targets, and massive marketing budgets.

Food companies also spend tons of money engineering the perfect level of sweetness to addict you and the perfect feel in your mouth to keep you coming back for more of this unhealthy crap. Healthy people don't eat a lot of food that requires scientists and engineers to make it taste good. They generally choose foods that Nature made taste good.

If your goal is to feel good, function optimally, and have an amazing life, you have to start making decisions based on what is best for your physical, mental, emotional, and spiritual health.

## EVERY SINGLE THING YOU PUT IN YOUR BODY HAS AN EFFECT ON YOU.

*Everything.* Some of those effects may be unintended, like in the case of pharmaceutical "side effects." Those "side effects" are really just effects that the pharmaceutical company wishes didn't happen when you took the drug, but everything you put in your body affects you in some way at some point in time.

Choose consciously. Think about the effects of what you are putting in your body. What will it do to your mood? To your attitude? To your vibration? To your overall state of being? Feeling great is the goal. Because when you feel great, it's a lot easier to manifest the life of your dreams than when you're focusing all of your attention on dealing with health problems. Make choices that support the best and healthiest version of you.

## Easy Ways to Clean Up Your Diet

*You are What You Eat: Exchange Food-Like Substances for Actual Food.*

Jake started embodying health with one single decision: to stop eating four Pop-Tarts and drinking Dr Pepper for breakfast every day.

He had abs, but he was still eating like crap. One day, it just hit him—maybe Pop-Tarts and Dr Pepper weren't the best choices for the "most important meal of the day." So, he traded them for scrambled eggs and instant oatmeal. One choice at a time, he went from eating crap to eating healthy.

It didn't happen overnight. He went from picking better fast-food choices to eventually cooking all his own whole food. He realized the truth of the cliché "you are what you eat." Your cells are literally replacing themselves with the raw materials you're feeding into your body.

As Jake always tells people: "You wouldn't put maple syrup in your car and expect it to run right. Your body is your vehicle, and you have to put in the right fuel in order for it to run correctly."

This is why I know what Jake says works. He doesn't just talk the talk. He walks the walk. After we moved in together, I got a front-row seat to watching someone live, eat, cook, and be healthy... every single day, all day long. Talk about a priceless gift.

Fast food, junk food, and processed food qualify as food-like substances. Real food is whole food: meat, fish, rice, grains, vegetables, fruits, nuts, etc. Whole foods are a key to health. Eat *real food*. Not food-like substances or something that involved scientists, engineers, and a lab.

Watching Jake taught me that healthy people shop differently in the grocery store. They don't go down the aisles in the middle very often. When we grocery shop these days, our first stop is organic produce, then grass-fed organic meat or low-mercury, wild-caught fish. Next, we head to the organic section for rice, oats, other clean carbs, and spices. Finally, we grab organic, vegetarian-fed free-range eggs and organic unsweetened almond milk, and we're out the door. Jake always has a list, pretty much sticks to it completely, doesn't shop off the end caps, and is 100 percent unemotional about his food choices.

Watching Jake also taught me that healthy people don't buy food in the grocery store without reading the ingredients list first. What's more, healthy people mostly choose foods that don't have an ingredients list. The food *is* the ingredient.

The better your choices, the healthier you become.

Plus, a pro tip from Jake:

**IF YOU DON'T BUY IT, IT'S NOT IN YOUR HOUSE WHEN YOU'RE HUNGRY AND MIGHT BE TEMPTED TO EAT IT. YOU CAN'T EAT WHAT'S NOT THERE. STEP 1: STOP BUYING IT.**

### *Cook as Much of Your Own Food as Possible*

When you cook your own food, you are in control. You decide what you make, what goes in it, how it's cooked, and how healthy it is. As Jake says, you're only as healthy as the person cooking your food.

Also, this is important: Cook with *love*, not haste.

I didn't understand this for years. Jake would always hand me plates of food and tell me it was cooked with love and I thought it was something he just said. It wasn't. He actually thinks about and consciously radiates the frequency of *love* into the food he cooks while he's cooking it. It might sound wild to you, but this is a real thing.

When you cook with haste, you're emitting that electromagnetic frequency, and it's being absorbed by the food that you're cooking. Whenever I would cook, which I didn't used to enjoy, Jake would say to me, "This was cooked in haste, not with love." He could literally tell from how it tasted.

Takeout and restaurant food may taste great, but you're not just feeding your taste buds. You're a collection of trillions of cells.

You're feeding every cell in your body. What you feed them dictates how well they function, and how well they function determines your overall health.

Think about how much salt and butter and who knows what else restaurants put it their food to make it taste great. It's likely you would *not* prepare your food the same way at home. After all, restaurants mostly only care about taste, keeping food costs low to make a profit, and keeping you coming back for more. Most don't truly care about your health at all, and most can't afford to use organic produce, organic grass-fed meats, and wild-caught low-mercury fish.

Healthy people prepare most of their own food.

### Drink Water

One of the first pieces of advice Jake gave me was one he gives everyone:

**TRY TO DRINK A GALLON OF UNFLAVORED FILTERED WATER EVERY DAY.**

Your body is primarily made of water. You need water to survive. Also, you have no idea how many of the "issues" you're dealing with are due to dehydration. Jake says, "Drink a glass of water before you come at me." You are not your best self when you're dehydrated.

Don't be surprised if you lose weight when you start drinking lots of water. The more water you drink, the less water weight your body holds because it learns that it has a continuous supply coming. If you don't like the taste of water, you can learn to like it. After all, think of how many people have learned to like the taste of beer.

Also, we don't care what your dentist or TV says, fluoride is not good for you. It's a toxin and exposure is associated with many health conditions, including: acne, bone weakness, bone cancer, cardiac failure, diabetes, early puberty in girls, harm to the fetal brain, hypertension, insomnia, lower fertility rates, lower IQ, neurotoxic effects (including ADHD, osteoarthritis, thyroid disfunction, and more.[2] Make sure you're filtering all fluoride out of your water, especially if you live in a city.

Also, something we had no idea about until we started reading *Estrogeneration: How Estrogenics Are Making You Fat, Sick, and Infertile* by Dr. Anthony G. Jay: If you live in an area that practices water reclamation, don't drink the tap water.[3] Water reclamation is the process by which they turn pee into drinking water. They may be able to filter out a lot of the nasty crap, but they can't filter out the hormones.[4]

If you want a giant dose of estrogen, drink some tap water in south Florida. Yuck.

### Think About Nature When You're Choosing Your Food

Wild animals are generally wildly healthy. They have to be, or they die.

One of the funniest realizations I ever came to was when Jake told me that no wild animal in nature is out there drinking another animal's milk as an adult. Only humans do that. It struck me as *super weird* that humans were the only species out there drinking milk as adults, especially of another species.

Quitting dairy has incredible health benefits, less systemic inflammation and less mucus being two of the big ones.

Here's another really good reason to quit dairy: one of the casomorphins in cow's milk is "associated with disruptive brain functioning and neurological disorders, such as autism and schizophrenia."[5] We've never been healthier since becoming a dairy-free household.

Also, if you're worried about where you're going to get your calcium, milk isn't a very good source to begin with[6]—it just had great marketing. Only 30 percent of the calcium per serving of milk can even be absorbed by the body.[7] Try dark leafy vegetables, sesame seeds, almonds, and broccoli instead—they're way better for you and some even have more calcium than milk.[8]

You know what else wild animals avoid? Poison. This is why we eat organic.

"The synthetic pesticides, fungicides, and herbicides used to treat conventionally grown food . . . are carcinogenic—and they negatively affect the microbiome and [the] gut lining."[9]

Also, most of the insecticides are neurological poisons.[10] "Researchers are now finding a strong connection between pesticides used to grow fruits, vegetables, and livestock feed, and virtually every dangerous illness."[11]

Even if you wash conventionally grown fruits and veggies, those carcinogenic toxins and poisons are still going in your body. You're eating what the plant absorbed too.

Researchers followed a family of five in Sweden who ate conventionally grown food for one week, followed by two weeks on organic food.[12] What happened? The family's urine tests revealed that "concentrations of selected pesticides decreased by 95% when the family switched to organic food."[13]

Close friends of ours recently switched to eating almost all organic due to pregnancy, and they were amazed at how much better they felt and how much better food tasted.

Organic food is awesome. Yes, it's more expensive, but if you're not eating at restaurants, ordering takeout, and buying food-like substances, the money part tends to even out more. Plus, your health is worth it. You don't even know how good you can feel until you try it.

We don't care who says that eating conventionally grown produce and factory-farmed meat is healthy; we don't do it anymore if we can help it. Our health is too important to knowingly eat toxins.

We also quit gluten because of the contamination from glyphosate, a very common herbicide used in America that has been banned in *many, many other countries*, the use of which (although not in food) has been linked by jury verdicts to causing cancer.[14] Herbicides like glyphosate are also endocrine system disruptors, and "[e]ven worse, they damage DNA, making cells age faster and become more susceptible to cancer."[15] Also, another reason to quit gluten comes from Dr. Tom O'Bryan: "There are no enzymes in humans that can fully digest the gluten proteins found in wheat, rye, and barley. These grains will cause inflammation and intestinal permeability every time they are eaten."[16] Microtears in your intestines aren't cool for anyone.

Another thing wild animals aren't big on if they're given a choice—GMOs. The deer around our house will choose non-GMO corn over GMO corn every chance they get.

We don't eat any genetically modified food anymore. Ann Boroch, a certified nutritional consultant and naturopath, says in *The Candida Cure*:

Genetically altered foods are filled with herbicides, which can damage our bodies. Studies link GMOs to kidney and liver damage, allergies, gastric disturbances, and cancer. Eighty percent of US corn and soy is genetically modified, and GMO corn is the base that we are using to feed all non-organic livestock and fish.[17]

If someone says GMOs are good for you or don't impact your health, they're either ignorant of these facts, or you should probably check to see what kind of financial ties they have to the GMO food industry. Food and seed companies lobbied so heavily and spent so much money that they were able to successfully block laws from being made that would require the labeling of GMO foods in the United States, despite the fact that consumers seem overwhelmingly in favor of them.[18]

This is big business and big money, and it almost certainly has nothing to do with improving *your health*. Where big profits are at stake, most companies don't really care what the food is actually doing to your body.

If you can't afford to eat all organic, or simply want to know what to avoid, here's a list of foods that are commonly GMO, provided by the NONGMO Project.

### High Risk Crops
Corn, soy, canola, cotton, sugar beets, alfalfa, papaya, potato, zucchini, and summer squash.

### Animal Products
Eggs, milk, honey, seafood, meat.

### Processed Inputs
Corn syrup, flavorings, hydrolyzed and vegetable protein, molasses, sucrose, vitamins, and genetically engineered microbes (referred to as synthetic biology), such as yeast and algae, to produce enzymes, fats, flavors, oils, sweeteners, and milk and egg proteins.

### Monitored Crops
*(at risk of contamination from existing GMOs or are known to have GMO varieties in development)*
Apple, camelina, flax, mushroom, mustard, orange, pineapple, rice, salmon, sugarcane, tomato, wheat, turnip, bok choy, chard, rutabaga, table beets, and varieties of squash.[19]

## *Quit Drinking Alcohol*

The societal programming around alcohol is incredibly prominent and strong. You see it in movies, on TV, in advertisements, with celebrity alcohol companies and endorsements, and more.

But here's the truth:

**ALCOHOL IS TERRIBLE FOR YOU.**

It dramatically lowers your vibration and it takes a while for you to be able to climb back up the vibrational scale. Plus, as Jake learned in his drinking and driving classes after he lost his license for his second DWI, alcohol is the only drug that negatively affects every organ and system in your body. "All alcohol is a neurotoxin that goes directly into the bloodstream, creates an inflammatory response, and depletes vitamins and minerals in your body," according to Ann Boroch.[20]

Our choice is not to drink at all. We choose cannabis over alcohol every day of the week. Did you know your body actually has an endocannabinoid receptor system, and it's the largest receptor system in your body?[21]

The endocannabinoid receptor system has "no receptors in the cardiac and respiratory centers of the brainstem, the areas that shut down the heart and lungs in cases of overdose. This is the physiological reason no one has ever died of a cannabis overdose, and why it is one of the safest, if not the safest, medicine on earth."[22]

An average person would have to smoke more than fifteen hundred pounds of cannabis (twenty to forty thousand joints) in fifteen minutes to ingest the amount that would kill 50 percent of people (known as the LD50).[23] Ironically, cannabis is still considered a Schedule I drug with "no therapeutic value" by the federal government, despite the fact that the US government has owned a patent on "cannabinoids as antioxidants and neuroprotectants since 2003."[24]

Plus, your brain actually makes a chemical that mirrors the effects of THC and has a very similar chemical structure.[25] It was discovered in 1992 by Dr. Raphael Mechoulam and is called anadamide, based on the Sanskrit word anada, which means *"bliss."*[26]

You know what your body doesn't have? An alcohol receptor system.

### *Spend a Few Months Learning to Eat Healthy*

Another thing I learned from Jake is that when you decide to get healthy or fit, the first thing you need to do is go to the grocery store and learn how to read labels and choose healthy food.

Before you buy anything, turn it over and read the ingredients. If you can't pronounce them and don't know what they are, there's a good chance you don't want to put them in your body. But to make sure, look them up on your smart phone while you're standing there.

The goal is eventually to eat mostly only unprocessed foods that don't come with ingredients lists, but we know transitioning from the standard American diet to a healthy diet is a process best done in stages. You'll get there. It's one step at a time.

To reiterate one of Jake's pro tips:

### TAKE STEPS TO AVOID TEMPTATION.

Jake had to completely change his routine in order to quit buying candy, because if he saw, he bought it. To break this habit, he avoided all convenience stores and switched to only paying at the pump. He also would only pay in grocery store lines that had no candy at the checkout, even if that meant walking over to the service desk or liquor section. When he stopped buying it, he didn't eat it. As time went on, his addiction to sugar dissipated.

Take your time learning about how to eat healthy. Read books about it. Do research. Take a good three months to just work on your diet and clean it up. The changes don't all have to be made overnight, and you don't have to quit everything at once. When you can emotionally handle letting certain foods go, do it. You *are* going to end up giving stuff up. But remember, you're not doing it as a punishment. You're doing it to give yourself the gift of vibrant health, which feels so much better than anything could ever taste. You just have to experience feeling the benefits so you know the truth.

## Gut Health and Your Microbiome

It wasn't until I took responsibility for my own health, that I even learned the word *microbiome*. I had no idea it was your gut or that it was so wildly important. Did you know that over 80 percent of your serotonin is made in your gut?[27] Your mental health isn't really in your head, it's in your gut. Did you know that 70 percent of your immune system is also in your gut?[28] If you have an unhealthy gut, you have an unhealthy system. And what affects your gut? *Everything you consume.*

"The composition of the microbiome—based on the food you eat—can shape a healthy immune response or predispose you to disease."[29]

Sick of feeling tired, irritable, annoyed, cranky, depressed, lethargic, anxious, and many other things you don't want to feel anymore? Get serious about your gut health. Your intestinal wall lining is one cell thick.[30] *One cell.* If you eat something that your body is sensitive to or doesn't like, you get a microtear in that lining, and then all that stuff going through your intestines has a hole where it can sneak out into your body and trigger all sorts of responses that aren't beneficial for you.[31]

"Every system of your body improves when your gut functions more normally," according to Dr. Tom O'Bryan in *You Can Fix Your Brain*, a fabulous book that explains so well why gut health is wildly important to your mental health.[32] I learned this truth firsthand through my own personal experience. Healing my gut restored my mental health—and so quickly too!

Here's another great fact to know:

Learning about your microbiome and how to take care of it can completely change your life, not to mention erase many health problems you may be facing. It's not complicated. It's not scary. It's really empowering information that you can use to live a healthier, better life.

You can take a food sensitivity test that will tell you what types of foods might be tearing that single-cell thick intestinal wall lining.

You can take a gut health test that will tell you what kind of microbes are primarily found in your gut, whether or not they're the good ones, and what to feed your body to improve your microbiome. Knowledge is power, as are the resources we've included at the end of the chapter.

Also, don't be surprised if your doctor doesn't know much, or anything at all, about the microbiome. In general, it takes almost twenty years for basic science research to make it into your regular doctor's office.[33]

Becoming your own advocate, doing your own research, and taking responsibility for improving your own health is more important now than ever before. There's no question that many traditional medicine doctors are falling behind on the knowledge and research that can help heal you. But you don't have to wait for them to catch up. You can start becoming healthier any moment you want.

Check out the books and documentaries we've listed at the end of this chapter, and feel what calls to you. They've all been instrumental in restoring my health, and Jake and I are both so grateful to every single one of the creators.

Bottom line:

**YOUR HEALTH IS YOUR RESPONSIBILITY, AND GUT HEALTH IS HEALTH.**

We can't stress enough how powerful it is to learn about your microbiome and how to take care of it. The knowledge can change how you think about everything you put in your body. Here are some really important things we learned about how to protect and care for it.

### *Avoid Antibiotics Whenever Possible*

Antibiotics destroy your gut health because they wipe out both the good and bad microbes.[34]

Sometimes antibiotics are unavoidable and truly necessary for your health or to save your life. But when you understand how devastating they are to your gut health and your overall health, you'll generally only use them in situations where they are truly necessary or life-preserving.

## NOTHING WILL DESTROY YOUR GUT HEALTH FASTER THAN TAKING ANTIBIOTICS.

In hindsight, it's not surprising that I had crappy mental health when I was taking doxycycline every day for cystic acne that came about as a result of a birth control implant. I wish I had never taken antibiotics for trivial stuff like that. It truly was not worth the consequences to my health, but at the time, I had no idea of the impact of antibiotics on my gut.

Now you do, so you can make more informed choices.

### *Avoid Taking Pharmaceuticals Whenever Possible*

Pharmaceuticals have many, many unintended effects on your body and your health. Have you ever had to get a second prescription to address the "side effects" of your first one?

It's a thing, and it's dangerous.

Cleaning up your diet and living a healthy lifestyle will do more for your health than pharmaceuticals will probably ever be able to do. Vibrant health does not come in a pill bottle. I tried. It never materialized.

Pharmaceuticals also impact your microbiome. How, we can't say exactly, because we don't know if pharmaceutical companies are spending any money on that kind of research. They tend to spend a lot of their money on marketing.

Which, side note, did you know that the United States and New Zealand are the only two countries in the world where it's currently legal for pharmaceutical companies to advertise directly to consumers with product claims?[35] We didn't either until we looked it up. What's more, we were shocked to learn that it's not unusual for pharmaceutical companies to spend more money on marketing than on research and development.[36]

That just seems odd, doesn't it? Or maybe not, considering pharmaceutical companies are simply for-profit corporations ultimately beholden legally to their shareholders, who no doubt love bigger profits. A patient cured is a customer lost.

We're not saying to ditch all of your pharmaceuticals, especially without consultation with a medical professional.

We understand how they can help you. Sometimes, it's the only thing giving you relief so you can function. But you need to be aware that they are impacting your body in ways you might not fully understand right now (and your doctor probably doesn't either. The healthier your lifestyle, the higher the probability becomes that you may not need the drugs you once thought you couldn't live a single day without.

I'm living proof. No doctor believed it was possible for me to survive without prescription medication. But when I took control of my own health, changes beyond anything I could ever imagine happened. When I was willing to change my lifestyle, I got truly healthy.

And when you're truly healthy, pharmaceuticals just aren't part of your life very often.

### *Avoid Over-the-Counter Medicine Whenever Possible*

Whether it's a pain reliever or an antacid, they can have real implications for your gut health.[37]

It seems like they should be harmless since you're able to buy them with your groceries, but they're not. What's more, when you're truly healthy, you don't need them because you don't have the symptoms they're meant to control unless you're involved in some kind of accident or trauma.

I haven't popped an over-the-counter pill in over three years—and who knows how long Jake has gone without one. We choose to treat any issues that we encounter with natural alternatives like food; supplements; herbal, homeopathic, or natural remedies; meditation; or acupuncture—things that don't harm our microbiome.

We're very choosy about what we put in our bodies because we know that everything we consume has an effect on us, and we value feeling great every day.

### *Try to Eat All the Colors of the Rainbow*

We learned this, and so much more, from a wonderful documentary series called *The Interconnected Series: The Power to Heal from Within* by Dr. Pedram Shojai. Watching it was life-changing, and we highly recommend it.

When you eat a varied diet of whole foods and all the colors of the rainbow in fruits and vegetables every day, you're feeding a broader spectrum of gut microbes that you need to become and stay healthy. What you eat determines the microbes in your gut that you're feeding and what you feed grows.

Make sure it's the good microbes that leads to positive health outcomes.

### Quit Eating Sugar

Sugar is more addictive than cocaine, yet it's socially acceptable and legal to sell to children. We've done both, and from personal experience, there is no comparison of how hard it is to quit sugar versus quitting cocaine. Quitting sugar was much harder to do.

Sugar has zero nutritional value. There is literally no reason to put it in your body. It alters your taste buds, negatively affects your health in pretty much every single way you can't even imagine, affects your mood, and leads to all sorts of bad outcomes.

"Eating processed sugar increases systemic inflammation. In fact, refined sugar is one of the most inflammatory foods in any quantity," according to Dr. Tom O'Bryan.[38] "Without sugar, you may find that many of your emotional problems, including anxiousness, depression, and irritability, may dissipate. It's that simple."[39]

Sugar is garbage. And not just sugar, you also have to watch out for high fructose corn syrup, fruit juice concentrates, artificial sweeteners, sugar substitutes, and more.

Sugar feeds microbes in your gut that leads to negative health outcomes. Those microbes protest when you quit feeding them because they are *starving*. Like any living organism, they don't want to die.

This is why you get sugar cravings. These microbes want to be fed so they can keep living and growing.

But you don't want that. Don't give in. Quit feeding them. You're stronger than the cravings. Once you've been off sugar for a while, your body and gut will change and you won't crave sugar anymore.

Plus, there's an awesome bonus—after you quit sugar, your taste buds change and everything else tastes *so much better*. That fruit that didn't seem sweet enough to satisfy your craving will taste better than it's ever tasted in your life.

However, if you can't quit sugar 100 percent, you will still do yourself a massive favor by reducing it drastically in your diet. Read labels to ensure you know all the hidden places it pops up in like ketchup, marinades, and 85 percent of the foods in a normal grocery store.[40] Be mindful of how you feel after consuming products with sugar. If you're paying attention, you'll notice how it affects your mind, body, mood, and overall state of being.

Reducing or quitting sugar can be one of the best things you ever do for your health and happiness. It has been for us.

**Get Moving**

As Jake constantly tells me and everyone else, "an object in motion stays in motion." When you move, you feel more alive. So, move your body simply for the joy of moving it, not because you're punishing yourself with exercise. Find something active you enjoy doing. It doesn't have to be what anyone else enjoys. It could be lifting weights, ballroom dancing, tae kwon do, playing hopscotch, competitive lawn mowing . . . it truly doesn't matter. Just *move.* Be active. This is an integral part of living a healthy lifestyle.

And here's a bonus: the more you move, the more calories you burn, and the more food you can eat without it affecting your physique.

But here's the real reason I started moving every day: fifteen to thirty minutes of cardiovascular activity—just getting your heart rate up—has been proven more effective than antidepressants in studies. A wonderful doctor told me that, and I confirmed it with my own personal experience.

After fifteen years on those useless pills that were *never* going to cure my depression (which another doctor *finally* told me), I changed my lifestyle to prioritize health and happiness above all. I quit antidepressants *forever*, and I've never been more filled with joy and love in my life—joy and love I could never have felt if I were still chemically altering my mental state with antidepressants.

Bottom line:

## YOU DON'T NEED TO MAKE FITNESS YOUR WHOLE LIFE TO BE HEALTHY, YOU JUST NEED TO MAKE BEING ACTIVE A MUST IN YOUR LIFE.

A consistent must until it becomes a habit. And once it's a habit, you'll probably never be able to imagine your life without it, because you love how you feel so much.

Get moving. It can change your life.

## Avoiding Toxins and Detoxing

At present, we live in a toxic world. Our air, water, soil, and food supply have all been tainted. But you can do a great job avoiding toxins and detoxing from them with a little knowledge, awareness, and effort.

An easy place to start is with your food. We've already covered eating organic, non-GMO, and quitting gluten. Step one to avoiding toxins: make sure you're not consuming them in everything you eat.

Another easy way to avoid toxins is to be mindful of what you have in your home. Exchange plastic for glass to get rid of BPA, which is an endocrine disruptor that causes all sorts of problems.[41] Don't ever microwave food in plastic containers, don't use plastic wrap on your food, don't drink out of plastic water bottles made from BPA, as it may have leeched into the water, and try not to touch receipts printed using thermal paper.[42]

Also, just because something is BPA-free doesn't necessarily make it better. Dr. Tom O'Bryan taught us that BPF is usually substituted instead, and that's even worse.[43]

Look at your cleaning products and switch them out for nontoxic versions. You don't need that stuff absorbing through your skin or being inhaled as you breathe.

Also, check and see how many products in your home have artificial fragrance. Artificial fragrances generally contain phthalates, which are endocrine disruptors[44] and "are carcinogenic and known to cause reproductive damage."[45] This includes phthalates and artificial fragrances in *all products*, not just air fresheners, colognes, perfumes, body sprays, and hair and beauty products. They might smell pretty, but they are not good for you.

We also avoid anything with artificial dyes, colors, and flavorings, as those are problematic as well.

Be smart when eating fish and seafood too. I ended up with extremely high toxic levels of mercury as well as arsenic in my body that had to be detoxed. Heavy metal toxicity is no joke. It can totally make you feel like you're straight-up crazy and give you all sorts of other gnarly symptoms. Have you ever heard the phrase *mad as a hatter*? Hats used to be dipped in mercury, and the exposure would make the person creating them act nuts.

I also had all my mercury fillings removed, which you should only have done after consultation with a medical professional who understands the safest way to help you through it. I took detox supplements before and after the procedure, and even then, there were some bumpy moments as the mercury was leaving my system.

Heavy metals are serious toxins, and we highly recommend getting properly tested for them—and mycotoxins from mold—by a medical professional, if you're having health issues that don't seem to be going away, you research and identify with any symptoms, or you think you've been exposed.

The best option is to find a healthcare professional who is open-minded and preferably has detoxed from these personally. If you need to detox, you really want someone who has been through the process and can give you accurate and helpful guidance on the easiest and gentlest way possible. The last thing you want is to force your cells to release a bunch of toxins into your system, make you feel *absolutely terrible and crazy*, and potentially harm your body.

Not all healthcare professionals are open-minded. Try a functional medicine doctor (you can find one on www.ifm.org), a naturopath, an enlightened DO, or an MD who has woken up to the reality and limitations of conventional medicine. There are healthcare professionals out there who will listen to you and won't just say *this is in your head* or shove prescriptions at you. You just have to find one who really believes in holistic healing—not just treating symptoms.

To detox naturally every single day, we incorporate healing foods into our diet. You'd be amazed how much you can reduce your toxic load by adding cilantro, wild blueberries, spirulina, and atlantic dulse to your diet.[46] High-quality herbs and supplements are also a great way to detox, as is drinking tons of filtered water. Your body loves to pass all this toxic garbage out through your pee, poop, and sweat.

But remember, not all of the things you need to avoid are visible. One thing that people don't often think about as being problematic is EMF (electromagnetic field) pollution. We're constantly swimming in an EMF soup, unless you take steps to moderate your exposure.

In order to try to shield ourselves from the damage done by EMF pollution we have personally taken the following steps in our life and home:

- Removing EMF-producing devices from our bedroom (including our cell phones)
- Not using cell phones when they're plugged in (which increases the EMF impact)
- Drastically limiting our time on cellphones and computers
- Removing our SmartTV from our home
- Putting our cell phones on airplane mode overnight
- Taking our WiFi router out of our bedroom (did you know seeds often won't germinate next to one?)
- Plugging our WiFi router into a timer that shuts off around the time we go to bed
- Choosing not to allow a Smart Meter to be installed on our home.

People who stay overnight at our house always seem to have the best night's sleep that they've had in recent memory. Jake maintains it's because we're not sleeping with the WiFi on, and I agree with him, especially after I spent a week at a hotel recently.

We live out in the middle of nowhere, so we don't pick up anyone else's WiFi networks. At the hotel, I couldn't get away from them. We know our bodies really don't like EMF pollution, so we're much more aware of it, and we take steps to avoid it as much as possible.

If you live in a city or in an apartment or condo building, you're inundated with WiFi and EMF pollution beyond anything Jake or I experience living out in the boonies. EMF pollution has been proven to have a negative effect on your health, including causing anxiety, concentration difficulties, depression, fatigue, headaches, memory impairment, nausea, palpitations, and sleep disturbances.[47]

There's a lot to know about avoiding toxins and even invisible EMF pollution in our currently toxic and polluted world, but you can learn this stuff and adjust your lifestyle if you see fit, how you see fit, and when you see fit.

No one is going to do this for you or make you change the way you live so you're exposed to fewer toxins and less pollution. No one else is really looking out for your health on this one. This is research you have to do yourself and choices you have to make yourself—for *yourself.*

When you do your own research, you learn things like: in Europe, chemicals have to be proven safe before they can be used in consumer products. Not in America. If you want to read something chilling, start researching all the chemicals that have been banned in Europe that are still perfectly legal and are commonly used in the United States.

But you're smart, and you can learn about this stuff and adjust what needs adjusting in your life. Then it's just one more puzzle piece you snap into place to create your picture of vibrant health.

**Embrace the Suck**

Embracing the suck is a big part of transitioning to a healthy lifestyle. The rewards are exponentially better than the suck, but you have to get through the transition to appreciate them. And the only way to do that . . . is to do it.

As Jake says, "It's like baking a cake. You have to put in some time in the oven. The oven isn't a comfortable place. Do you think being in a cocoon is fun for a caterpillar? Its organs are literally breaking down and its cells are receiving new instructions on how to reform. Transformation sucks. You only enjoy the process after you've seen the reward."

One day you can just feel the difference. Then you look back and realize how far you've come. You have the power to transform your entire life by choosing to be healthy and active. Health consciousness happens one choice at a time.

> **Do I eat this or that?**
> **Do I get up and move or make an excuse**
> **and stay in bed or on the couch?**
> **Do I stop using my favorite product because**
> **I now know it contains toxins?**
> **Do I make choices today that will put me on the**
> **path to better future outcomes?**

I don't know who said this, but it's one of the truest statements I've ever read: "If you do not make time for health, you will be forced to make time for illness." Either you invest in yourself and your health now, or you pay the piper later.

Health seems like a big investment until you're doing it, and then you can't imagine living any other way. The choices get easier. They become a habit you don't even have to think about anymore, because you're simply acting from the consciousness of health. It becomes who you are. You embody it.

Then magically, you like how you feel. You like how you look. You like who you are. You love yourself more. You have more confidence. You raise your vibration. You attract more awesome things into your life and everything gets even better.

## HEALTH. IS. MAGICAL.

This may not be an incentive you've heard about before to get healthy, but it's what Jake and I have both personally experienced on our own health journeys—we found happiness.

I started caring about my health when my mental health was crap and all I wanted was to be happy again. Getting healthy is the fastest and most sustainable path to happiness that we've ever encountered. It's a magical way to live.

I never feel deprived. I feel incredible—strong, confident, and more in love with myself, my body, and my life than ever before. The rewards were so wonderful that I didn't even know it was possible to live this way. But Jake did, *of course*.

But first, you have to *do it*. For yourself. That's the only way it happens. You can't be pushed, prodded, shamed, or forced into health. You have to decide that you want to be healthy. And then you have to stop talking about it, and start being about it. Only you can choose.

Also, another bonus I totally didn't expect from becoming healthy and more in tune with my body was this:

### MY INTUITION IS SO MUCH STRONGER NOW.

I didn't know there was a connection here, but Jake did. Getting in tune with your body—which is way easier when you're healthy and not running tons of drugs, toxins, and crap through your system—is a great way to enhance your connection to the Divine. It's so much easier to feel and recognize those intuitive hits and nudges so you can take aligned and inspired action leading you to the life of your dreams.

Finally, a tip on losing weight:

### STOP SAYING, "I'M TRYING TO LOSE WEIGHT."

Why? You'll always be expressing the consciousness of someone who is trying to lose weight.

### INSTEAD, TRY SAYING, "I'M GETTING HEALTHY."

This leads to a consciousness of health because health is the lens you're running your decisions through. The weight takes care of itself when you're living a healthy and active lifestyle.

Also, your weight is largely an irrelevant number and in no way should be running your life. Weight matters a lot more when you're shipping packages and freight. You're not freight. You'd be better off throwing out your bathroom scale and buying a food scale. It's much more important to know how much the food weighs that you're putting in your body than knowing how much your body weighs at a snapshot moment in time.

Your weight is not a good number to measure your health progress by either. Use your mirror. How do you look? How do you feel? Take pictures and then compare them if you want to see your progress.

**YOU ARE SO MUCH MORE THAN A NUMBER ON A SCALE. DON'T LET IT RUN YOUR LIFE.**

Neither Jake nor I have weighed ourselves in nearly two years. Neither of us cares what we weigh because we love the way we look and the way we feel, and that's so much more important than a silly number on a scale.

Obviously, this chapter isn't meant to be an exhaustive discussion on health. These are just some of the things that we, as people devoted to living a healthy, clean lifestyle think about and consider on a daily basis as we're making our decisions. This is part of our consciousness of health that we're sharing with you.

There is so much useful information out there and many, many wonderful experts who can give you even more assistance on details and particulars. For more information on all of these topics, here are some great books to read and documentaries to watch to continue expanding your powerful knowledge and consciousness of health:

*You Can Fix Your Brain* by Dr. Tom O'Bryan
*The Autoimmune Fix* by Dr. Tom O'Bryan
*The Toxin Solution* by Dr. Joseph Pizzorno
*The Candida Cure* by Ann Boroch
*The Biology of Belief* by Dr. Bruce Lipton
*A Mind of Your Own* by Dr. Kelly Brogan
*You are the Placebo* by Dr. Joe Dispenza
*Becoming Supernatural* by Dr. Joe Dispenza
*Medical Medium Series* by Anthony William
*Heal*, directed by Kelly Noonan
*The Interconnected Series*, created by Dr. Pedram Shojai
*That Sugar Film*, directed by Damon Gameau

# ELEVEN
## WEALTH, SUCCESS, AND LIVING WELL

> "Success is not the key to happiness. Happiness is the key to success."
> – Buddha

"I hate money," Jake said as he drove our lifted Toyota 4Runner from Placencia Casino to our first beach house in Belize.

"You can't hate money. It's a tool. You use it," I replied, stunned that anyone could hate money, or that the thought had ever crossed someone's mind.

I'd certainly never thought such a thing, and I was on my way to becoming a millionaire at the age of thirty-three. All I knew was that money was awesome and made life way easier. The more you had, the easier things were.

Jake and I were the epitome of real-life *Rich Dad Poor Dad*. His dad took a lower paying-job at the factory to be there to coach Jake's Little League team. His parents worked different shifts so they could raise him themselves rather than have a babysitter do it. There wasn't often much extra to go around.

My dad, on the other hand, came from a long line of brilliant, hardworking, everyday entrepreneurs. He taught me about picking stocks when I was ten, the intricacies and considerations of careful life-goal setting when I was thirteen, and was giving me books like *The Millionaire Mind* and *The Millionaire Next Door* when I was in high school (which I didn't read because I was too busy reading romance). He took a massive risk and chased his dream of finally becoming a business owner by borrowing a million dollars from the bank and buying a company when I was fourteen. Being the youngest kid at home, I basically went to business school with my dad as he learned how to run his company and talked about it every night at dinner when he finally made it home. And then, not surprisingly, my parents picked out the business school they wanted me to attend for college.

Jake and I had lived completely different lives before the Universe brought us together. We had wildly different strengths and perspectives through which we viewed the world. That's how soul mates work—everyone brings something unique to the table. Where Jake was a health savant, I was ignorant and programmed by societal conditioning, stuck on the weight-loss yo-yo train, hating my body. He changed my life by giving me the consciousness of health, and I transformed completely as a result.

But God didn't send me to the table empty-handed. I brought the consciousness of wealth and success, and showed Jake what it took to become a self-made multimillionaire and build a successful business. Jake lived that journey with me.

When we moved in together, I absorbed how he thought, spoke, acted, and made decisions about health—and the consciousness of health seeped into my pores through osmosis. On the flip side, he lived my every decision, every thought process, nearly every word, and watched how hard I worked and what I believed about myself to become a successful multimillionaire. That experience changed him because he absorbed the consciousness of wealth and success by osmosis too.

Neither of us realized what was happening at the time, but I remember Jake quitting a "how to become a millionaire" type of online course when he realized he already knew what they were teaching from watching me. In hindsight, it was probably a bit like me hiring a fitness model to write a diet and workout plan for me, and realizing I already knew what to do and how to do it because I was learning from the real deal 24/7.

In the last chapter, we gave you a lot of powerful information to try to help you absorb the consciousness of health. In this chapter, we're offering you knowledge and power to help you absorb the consciousness of wealth and success.

## HAVING A CONSCIOUSNESS OF WEALTH IS NOT JUST ABOUT HAVING MONEY IN THE BANK. IT'S A MINDSET, AND YOU CAN TOTALLY ADOPT IT.

Wealthy is something you *are*. You have to live it, be it, feel it, think it, talk it, and know it.

If you want to be wealthy, the first thing you have to do is assess how you feel about money. Are you like old Jake, hating money because you never had enough, and it seemed like all the stress in your life was directly related to money or the lack thereof? Or working jobs you hate because you need the cash, making you resent it even more?

If that sounds like you, it's okay. There is *a lot* of societal conditioning out there around money. Tons. And most of it is not conditioning you to become a financially free individual living the life of your dreams with an abundance of money every day. But you can totally become that person anyway.

Like Jake and me, you probably picked up your consciousness of money from whoever raised you. Whoever you were watching and listening to during those all-important years of birth through age six has had a big influence on how money shows up in your life.

But don't blame them if you're not where you want to be. They only knew what they knew and could only act from the level of consciousness they had at the time. You have no idea what they were taught or told along the way that led to the outcomes you experienced. Forgive them, then move on to changing your consciousness around money if you need to.

We are not saying that you should love money itself more than anything, though. Love money for what it is—a tool to make your life easier. Be grateful you have it to buy what you need or to give it away to prosper others. But money, by itself, is not the goal.

**MONEY, BY ITSELF, SHOULD *NEVER* BE THE GOAL.**

The goal is to *live well*. To live *your best life*. To live with joy and happiness and abundance. The goal is to live from the heart and choose to spend your time doing things that give you joy and leave you feeling fulfilled—rather than living in fear and letting your bank account dictate the choices you get to make and the experiences you get to have.

That shift requires a change in thinking. You probably aren't surprised at this point, given that *everything* starts with a thought.

Let's change the way you think about money.

At its most basic level, money is simply energy. Money is Source, just like everything else, including you.

Infinite Intelligence knows you need money to live on this planet right now—because you're made out of Infinite Intelligence. It knows *everything* you need and want and desire because It hears your every thought and word. Source wants you to have an abundance of money. Source never wants you to be limited by something as simple as *money*.

After all, you can't really play the leading role you were born to play in the Divine Plan of love unfolding in your life if your attention is always focused on worrying about how you're going to pay your bills or stressing about being broke. Source wants you to have everything you need—and more—in abundance. Source is nothing if not generous.

If money isn't currently flowing in your life abundantly, it's not because the Universe forgot your share. It's sitting out there, waiting for you to unlock the door that's been holding back your abundant supply.

So, how do you open up the floodgates to your Divine inheritance as a joint heir to the universal treasure house so you can experience the generosity of Source firsthand?

First, let's all agree on the fact that money is just a tool. It will not change who you are. All it does is expand and magnify who *you already are*. If you're miserable before you're rich, you'll still be miserable after. You'll just be stressing about different things. Remember, you take yourself with you wherever you go, even if it's into a higher tax bracket.

If you were cheap before, then you'll still be cheap after. If you were generous before, then you'll still be generous after.

**MONEY JUST MAGNIFIES EVERYTHING ABOUT YOU—ALL YOUR STRENGTHS AND ALL YOUR WEAKNESSES.**

However, as Tom Bilyeu, a wealthy entrepreneur, once said in a speech I attended, "Money is even cooler than you think." I knew it was true when he said it, and I still know it today.

Money solves money problems. That's one of the coolest parts about it.

Think about it—how many of your problems would disappear if you had an abundance of money? Probably a lot of them.

Jake and I refer to these as money issues, which aren't really issues, because we've always got money. If that sounds like stuff rich people say, it's because it is. And if you want to join the club and live a life where your path is made easier by having all the funds you need and not having to stress about money, you're going to want to start thinking, speaking, and acting like a rich person.

And before you get triggered about "rich people," know that anything coming up is likely a result of the societal programming mentioned earlier—which loves to program negative things into your life like lack, limitation, hardship, money stress, and being broke. After all, if you suddenly became wealthy, you wouldn't need a lot of the products out there that have made other people really, really rich.

Think of all the credit card companies, finance companies, banks, anyone who loans money—including predatory payday loans, car title loans, check-cashing services, and other dodgy financial products. They get rich when part of the population stays poor.

That's not a win-win situation. It's a destructive situation that has done a number on humanity, turning us into haves and have-nots, and defining us according to our socio-economic status instead of seeing every single one of us as equal in the eyes of our Creator—which we always have been and always will be, on the most basic soul level.

It's time to take your power back and shake off all that bogus societal programming that's holding back your abundance. You were born into this life with the expectation that you would learn how to use your God-given powers to create an abundant life for yourself. These powers are innate within you and cannot be taken from you—ever.

Let's start here:

**THERE'S NOTHING WRONG WITH BEING RICH, REGARDLESS OF WHAT IT MIGHT BE TRENDY TO SAY OR WHO IT MIGHT BE TRENDY TO BLAME AT THE MOMENT.**

You know why? Because being *rich* is simply attaining a state of consciousness that *everyone* has the option and ability to attain, regardless of their starting point or current life circumstances.

Being rich is awesome. Having all the money you need and being financially free is one of the greatest gifts you can ever give yourself. And make no mistake, it is a gift *you give yourself*. No one else is going to do this for you, regardless of how many times you may have wished you were born a trust-fund kid or independently wealthy.

It's so much better when the abundance that flows into your life comes without strings or guilt, or you having to tap dance and live your life the way someone else wants you to live it in order for you to get that abundance.

I'll never forget the movie *Greedy* with Michael J. Fox. The old rich uncle could get his entire family to jump through hoops on a regular basis because they all wanted his money when he died. Do you want to jump through hoops for a rich old man to get your money? It may seem easier than taking the DIY approach, but it isn't.

You can't cut corners here. In order to have a truly abundant life where money is always flowing freely for all your needs and you always have more than enough to share with others, you have to attain the consciousness of wealth. Obtaining the money any other way—without having the consciousness for it—may result in a windfall that can't be sustained, leaving you broke again someday. And that's definitely not what you want.

Plus, keep in mind that when you're wealthy, you can help a lot more people than you can when you're broke. Every person you give money to, whether it's for a product, service, or purely a generous donation, is someone you're helping to prosper. Source loves to prosper others—and Source works through *individuals*, like you and me. Which means God prospers others *through us*. If you have nothing in your bank account, how can God use you effectively in the Divine Plan to help to others?

Source wants you to have money. Source wants to use you—through your generous impulses, and your very existence—to help unfold the Divine Plan.

Source is working through you when you get that generous impulse to tip your hairstylist $300 so she can buy the Christmas gift she wants to give her little girl. Or when you send a check to the local food bank. Or when you deliberately choose to shop at local small businesses. Or when you feel the urge to pay for the coffee of the person behind you at a drive-thru. Or when you increase your business with a particular vendor because you know they're struggling due to forces beyond their control. Or when you create a job for someone who was fired for standing up for their integrity.

The Universe works through us, but it needs to have something to work with. Source can only use you as a channel for as much money as you'll allow to come into your life.

So, how do you give the big *yes* to Source and start the flow in your direction?

Take everything you've learned about your thoughts, words, decisions, and emotions, and start applying it to money, which includes not thinking about how much you *don't have* or stressing about not having enough or feeling fear, animosity, or anything other than goodwill when you're paying your bills.

Let's revisit the movie theater example for a moment to illustrate why this matters so much, *especially* if you're in dire financial straits:

Spirit, the very energy and substance of All That Is, is constantly pouring through you and is all around you. But Spirit can only produce in your life what is on the film reel of your consciousness.

If you worry about money a lot, your film reel has a lot of frames devoted to money stress. When the light of Spirit pours through that film, it's going to produce a lot of scenes, experiences, and situations in your life that result in you feeling money stress. Because that's what you told Spirit you wanted your movie to be about—through your thoughts, words, beliefs, emotions, and actions. Your subconscious mind is always listening, remember?

Who actually wants a life featuring a heavy dose of money stress? No one we know.

But to change the movie and your life, you have to change the film reel—your consciousness.

You're never going to get rich while fearing you'll never have enough. To acquire a consciousness of wealth, you have to trade your fear for faith.

But how do you do that if you're in a tight financial spot and your outer reality shows the appearance of lack of funds? By thinking about the truth until you realize what it means for *you*.

> **SOURCE *IS* LAVISH ABUNDANCE.**
> **YOU ARE MADE *ONLY* FROM SOURCE.**
> **SOURCE LEFT *NOTHING OUT* WHEN YOU WERE MADE.**
> **THEREFORE, BECAUSE *YOU ARE SOURCE, YOU ARE ALSO LAVISH ABUNDANCE*. YOU ARE NATURALLY ABUNDANT.**
> **IT'S PART OF *WHO YOU REALLY ARE*.**

After all, Source would never incarnate as you without making sure you had abundance naturally built in. It's *Infinite Intelligence*. It wants to live an amazing life *through you*. Source knew it would need money in this incarnation, which is why you're always able to attract everything you need, if you can just get that film reel of your consciousness right.

You came into this life perfect, and if society and other people hadn't programmed fear and conditioning into you, you'd still be perfect. In fact, *you are still perfect*, under all those layers of fear and conditioning that you have to peel off and clear out to get back to your true nature.

Your true nature includes a consciousness of wealth.

If you hadn't been programmed otherwise, you would intuitively know that God always provides everything you need, at exactly the right time—or even before you need it. You can adopt this truth into your belief system and begin to act as though it's true at any moment. It's simply a shift of your mindset. However, it takes *faith* to believe this and act as if it's true until you experience the truth in your reality.

Once you experience the beautiful truth of abundance, you have solid proof that God really does provide for you when you need it. Then it becomes easier to have faith that it will always continue to be true, because abundance is your Divine birthright.

As you can see, it's a process of identifying and unlearning the unhelpful things that have been programmed into your belief system through your brain—which couldn't tell if the ideas were true or false at the time, through no fault of your own. And while it's not your fault that you've been programmed, it is your responsibility to deprogram yourself if you want to get on with living that awesome life the Divine intended for you when you incarnated.

It's natural and normal for you to be abundant. It's natural and normal for you to have all the money you need to play your constructive role in the Divine Plan of life.

All you have to do is start changing your words and worries about money into faith that God is never late and always finds a way—even if it's a way you didn't expect or know was possible.

Often, the Divine doesn't send cash to you directly. And while having it just appear in your bank account seems like the tidiest solution—and *it can happen*—sometimes the Universe is going to send you something even better.

An idea. A *brilliant* idea that you can turn into a business that gives you the gift of wealth.

If you're surprised, don't be. Creation is Spirit's jam. We were all *created to create*. It's hardwired into us to want to create things that didn't exist before.

It's also not surprising that a lot of rich people are business owners and entrepreneurs. Don't want to face a glass ceiling or limit on your income? Be your own boss, and no one gets to tell you how big your dreams and goals can be. *You* decide that.

If you're not into entrepreneurship and being a business owner, that's okay too. Source knows what is perfect for you, and will send you ideas and opportunities that will lead you in the right direction on your path.

It's time to surrender your fears around lack and limitation. Forgive yourself for them and forgive anyone else you have any kind of negative feeling toward for any reason about financial matters. Let it all go.

Start thinking new thoughts about money and pair them with new positive emotions. It will happen as a matter of degrees and realizations. Meditating on the truth helps you incorporate it into your mind and body.

You might know intellectually that abundance is what you truly are, but the trick is getting yourself to believe it on a soul-deep level. You have to *know it* and *be it* so Spirit can manifest it in your life.

Changing your consciousness is a process, but it's one you can totally excel at. You can start whenever you want, where you are, with what you have. The only limits are the ones you place upon life yourself.

### Digging Your Ditches

One of the very best in the business at "speaking the word" for financial demonstrations was Florence Scovel Shinn. In the *Game of Life and How to Play It*, Florence states:

> One of the greatest messages given to the race through the scriptures is that God is man's supply and that man can release, *through his spoken word*, all that belongs to him by divine right. He must, however, have *perfect faith in his spoken word*.
>
> Isaiah said, "My word shall not return unto me void, but shall accomplish that where unto it is sent." We know now, that words and thoughts are a tremendous vibratory force, ever moulding man's body and affairs.
>
> A woman came to me in great distress and said she was to be sued on the fifteenth of the month for three thousand dollars. She knew no way of getting the money and was in despair.

> I told her God was her supply, and that *there is a supply for every demand.*
>
> *So I spoke the word!* I gave thanks that the woman would receive three thousand dollars at the right time, in the right way. I told her she must have perfect faith, and act her *perfect faith.*[1]

The woman received the money through an extremely unexpected chain of events, at nearly the last moment. And as Florence says with her contagious faith, "Spirit is never too late."[2]

She also gives this advice: "Man must prepare for the thing he has asked for, *when there isn't the slightest sign of it in sight.*"[3] Florence calls this *digging your ditches*. You could also call this another case of faking it until you make it.

But how do you really *do it?* Florence says you must show *active faith*, taking steps as though what you need is already on its way to you.[4] This requires being fearless and shutting out all of your doubts. You can't think *of* the consciousness you want, you have to think *from* it.

If the money you need is already on the way to you, how would you feel? What would you do? Florence would tell you to feel and do those things *exactly*.

It's the same as when you're imagining the feeling of your wish fulfilled as you picture it while you're falling asleep. You're getting into character. You're feeling it as if it's real. You're already excited or joyful or grateful just like you would be when your dream comes true in your physical reality.

It's the same thing with *anything* you want to bring into your life, including money.

Imagine it. Feel how awesome it feels to get it. Remember: your body can't tell the difference! And then go about your waking hours with the assumption that what you've asked for—or something better—is already a done deal. Then you feel even more gratitude because you know it's already done on the invisible planes, and you're just waiting for the real world to catch up with what you already know is true.

As you can tell, this takes *faith*. Lots of faith. Unshakable faith.

You can't look at your bank balance and feel fear and doubt, wondering how you're going to make it stretch to cover everything. Look at that number and be grateful for what you have. Even better if you can celebrate when you see the number. Know that whatever it shows, God is taking care of the rest in perfect timing.

We know this might sound nuts, especially if you've got five dollars to your name, but it's the truth. Also, motivational speaker Tony Robbins has a great story he often tells about giving away the last five dollars he had so a boy could buy his mom lunch, and how it resulted in the Universe gifting him much, much more.

This stuff works. But in order for it to work, you have to work it and have faith.

When you pay bills, you can't be pissed about paying them or fearing that you're not going to have enough afterward. Pay your bills with joy that you're prospering another. This is totally a skill you can learn, regardless of how unnatural it may feel at the outset. And if you think you just can't learn to do that, know that we've finally graduated to sending our tax payments to the IRS with love. We didn't know that was possible—and it definitely didn't happen overnight. It's a process.

It helps that knowing money spent joyfully and with love returns to you multiplied. It doesn't matter what you're spending it on. You can feel joy and love about it if you can just find the right way to think about it. Plus, it's easier to feel joy about prospering others when you're spending your money with companies, businesses, and people you actually feel good about giving it to. We love shopping at small businesses, prospering our neighbors, members of our community, and companies with integrity.

## Creating Channels for Abundance

You need to help create channels for the Universe to prosper you through so you can receive even more abundance.

How do you do that?

One way is to stop thinking about your job as being the only means of supply that you have. It's not. God has ways we know not of and money can come from anywhere. But you have to believe it's possible in order to open up all of those infinite channels through which supply can make its way to you.

Remember when we talked about receiving gratefully? Sometimes abundance comes from places you don't expect. Be open to the Universe prospering you through any and all possible channels. Tell Source you accept and are open to receiving abundance on every level, from every possible means.

Then don't be surprised if you start to get hit with those good ideas. Like, the kind of idea that could turn into a multimillion-dollar business if you just focused some attention and thought on it and allowed it to grow.

This is literally how I became a millionaire. From ideas. Free ideas that just popped into my head as a gift from the Universe.

I didn't dismiss them as silly or stupid or impracticable. I embraced them. I gave them my attention. I spent my energy on them and allowed them to grow. I didn't let fear and doubt kill them. I had faith that those ideas could turn into something much bigger. And they did.

**YOUR WAY TO WEALTH IS ALREADY INSIDE YOU.**

It was built in as original equipment when you came into this incarnation. No one is missing this aspect from their soul journey, regardless of appearances to the contrary. You are meant to be abundantly supplied with all the material things you need to be a constructive part of the unfolding of the Divine Plan.

How do you tap into it?

Listen to the inspired ideas that pop into your head out of seemingly nowhere.

We're serious. This is for real. This is how God works and people find the right path.

If you're thinking—I've had these kinds of ideas! You're absolutely right. Source doesn't just give incredible ideas to special people. They're available to all of us. You just have to be willing to listen, trust, and put in some energy and effort to see where they lead.

Wealth doesn't just happen *to* you. It happens *through* you. It's the same as everything else—you are an inextricable part of the process and you have to play your role in the game. Your attention and energy are required ingredients in this recipe.

Sure, you can manifest lottery wins if you want. It's totally possible. But have you seen the stories about how lottery winners are generally broke again in a few years? That's because they got the money without acquiring the consciousness of wealth first. They couldn't hold on to the money because they didn't have the consciousness. It's a common story, because this stuff is law.

**ACQUIRE WEALTH CONSCIOUSNESS FIRST, AND THE MONEY TAKES CARE OF ITSELF.**

### Debt Slavery or Financial Freedom

What about debt?

Like I mentioned, I was raised on success consciousness, but I was also raised thinking there was nothing wrong with debt. After all, my father could never have achieved his dream of owning his own company without putting everything we owned—the house, the cars, and the business—in hock to the bank. I enjoyed an incredible childhood that was largely financed by debt.

Maybe you don't think debt is a problem either, and that's great.

But when you go so deep into debt that you can't quit the job that's killing your soul, you have become a debt slave.

I was one.

It wasn't until I was living paycheck to paycheck on $100,000 per year lawyer's salary that I finally understood what people meant by the phrase "golden handcuffs." Once I got the job with the big paycheck, my standard of living rose to fit my income, and then when I realized I hated the job, I couldn't quit because I'd financed *everything*.

I felt like I'd dug myself into a deep hole that I could never get out of. I had a brand-new house and mortgage (because mine had burned down), car payments, student loan payments, lines of credit, and more. I felt *trapped*. Debt was a weight around my neck that was dragging me under and suffocating me.

**AND THEN I REALIZED SOMETHING IMPORTANT.
IF I HAD NO DEBT, I COULD QUIT MY JOB AND DO SOMETHING I LOVED.**

Rather than write off that idea immediately as impossible, I thought about it. A lot.

Financial freedom became everything I wanted in my life, and I was willing to do anything to get there—including sell my new house and change my entire lifestyle.

I couldn't handle the thought of working a soul-draining job for the next however many years until I could finally retire, still a depressed, overweight, overstressed, overmedicated lawyer. That sounded like a fate worse than death to me.

At the time, I was prepared to take a 70 percent pay cut if I could just never be a lawyer again. But the Universe is nothing if not generous. It never required me to take a pay cut—*ever*.

Instead, Source gave me ideas. Lots of them.

I devoted all my free time to sorting through those ideas and finding the ones that excited me the most and felt the best when I mentally tried them on. Then I followed as the Universe led me to people and books that contained the knowledge and insight I needed to turn those ideas into reality. They changed my life by offering me invaluable advice that I applied to my books and my journey. And then eventually, the Universe led me down the perfect path to financial freedom.

But first, I had to ask for it in writing.

I still remember that day, sitting on my bed in a rental house, using my dad's great goal-setting insight as I wrote down that I wanted to make over a million dollars per year from writing books.

The very thought of it seemed *insane* at the time. Like, so insane, that I was never going to tell *anyone* I had written down that big of a goal.

My lips were *sealed*.

Despite how unrealistic it seemed at the time, I wrote it down anyway. I wrote down a *lot* of seemingly insane goals. I believed that despite how crazy they seemed, they could happen. Someday.

And then I went back to work, putting in over a hundred hours per week between my day job as a lawyer and trying to become a full-time author at night. I watched what *New York Times* best-selling authors did in my genre, and I emulated them—faking it in the beginning, like I mentioned earlier.

I reached out to them, asked them for advice, listened intently to what they said, read the books they suggested, and tried the things they told me to do. I learned to talk like them and to think like them. Then I started to become one of them. Until one day, I became not just their peer, but a rock star among them.

I had to grow into being the person for whom those insane dreams I'd written down could come true. Because that's how it works. You *grow into your dreams* by becoming the kind of person those dreams come true for.

The dream of becoming a financially free full-time author, doing what you love every day, only happens to someone who writes and publishes great books. In order for those dreams to become my reality, *I had to become that someone.*

This is how it works:

You don't become wealthy sitting on your couch smoking weed all day and daydreaming about how cool it would be if you never had to go to the job you hate ever again.

You have to become the person who wealth happens *through*.

You have to become the person who is listening for those brilliant ideas and intuitive nudges (which can totally happen when you're smoking weed too!).

You have to become the person who *acts* on those brilliant ideas and intuitive nudges.

You have to become the person who *believes* that those brilliant ideas and intuitive nudges are leading you to a wonderful life and great outcomes.

You have to *become the person* who the dreams you're dreaming can come true for.

You grow into becoming that person, and it only happens by changing who you are being—by changing your consciousness.

Success and wealth only happened to me because of who I was being. It only happened for me because of the consciousness I acquired.

I got to the point where I knew—with my whole heart and soul—that eventually my books would "break out" and I would become the rock star of an author I saw in my mind.

I *knew* this, and I believed it to the marrow of my bones and the depths of my soul.

I lived that belief. I acted on it.

I showed Florence's fearless faith, even when all I had was two flopped books and nothing but big goals and crazy dreams.

**DEEP DOWN, I KNEW IT WAS ONLY A
MATTER OF TIME BEFORE I SUCCEEDED.**

This was *key*. This was me knowing that what I wanted was not only possible for me, but that it *was going to happen for me*, and I lived my life accordingly. I became the person I needed to be long enough for those dreams to become my reality.

I was committed to keep going, no matter how long it took or how many books I had to write before it happened for me.

That kind of faith, belief, commitment, and conviction is powerful. It's the kind of faith, belief, commitment, and conviction that is unstoppable.

Why?

Because the Universe rewards complete faith, insane belief in yourself, determination, and daring. The Universe *loves* this stuff.

>Believe in yourself.
>Have faith.
>Listen to your ideas.
>Write them down.
>Give them your attention.
>Think about them.
>Feed them your energy.
>Keep them a secret.
>Listen to your intuitive nudges.
>Follow your heart.
>Have fun.
>See where your ideas lead.
>Set crazy goals.
>Write them down.
>Make the most of your opportunities.
>Enjoy yourself.
>Ask questions.
>Do your research.
>Be grateful for every bit of help you get along the way.
>Rest when you need it.
>Take a risk when it feels right.
>Make a bold move when you feel it in your gut.
>Don't get discouraged.

**Trust the process.
Keep the faith—you will be tested.
Be grateful for the journey and every part of it.
And again, *believe in yourself.*
*Believe that your dreams are possible for you.***

This is the kind of thinking and doing that leads to living an amazing life that you love that's flowing with abundance.

It's not just a bunch of wealth and success affirmations, which can help too. But wealth and success are so much more than saying, "I am wealthy" or "I am abundant" or "I am successful" over and over again. You have to *believe* in the abundance and generosity of the Universe.

If you need help believing this, take a look at the abundance of nature. It's undeniable how over-the-top abundant nature is. Then you have to know that Source wants you to be wealthy and successful. All that pure, perfect light is available to shine through and manifest whatever film you're playing on the reel of your consciousness.

You have to know that unlimited abundance is your true nature and that you have access to the universal treasure house where anything and everything you could ever want or need—and every experience you could ever want to experience—exists.

You have to *feel it*.

You have to *know it*.

It comes by degrees, and the more you think about it and experience realizations about the truth—those light-bulb moments that shift your consciousness—the faster it becomes your reality.

**YOU HAVE TO CHANGE WHO YOU ARE BEING BEFORE EVERYTHING ELSE CAN CHANGE AROUND YOU. IT'S LAW.**

Jake and I aren't wealthy because of the dollars in our bank account. We're wealthy because we feel wealthy. We always have enough. We always have enough to share. We always will have enough because God is our limitless supply, not our bank accounts.

The Universe can prosper us through any channel, and we love being delightfully surprised by where money can come from. We have faith that it'll keep coming. And as we spend it joyfully and use it to prosper others, we know we'll always be supplied with more to use because that's what Source intended for every single one of us.

Once you get your mind and beliefs right, the pieces start to fall into place.

Plus, we learned from Florence that money doesn't like to be stockpiled and hoarded in savings accounts and not used. Money is meant to be circulated. Florence tells us that "[t]he law always stands back of the man who spends fearlessly, with wisdom," especially in pursuit of a hunch, which is what she calls intuitive nudges or ideas.[5]

From my personal experience, I know that spending fearlessly—not carelessly, wastefully, pointlessly, or gambling—works. I've lived it.

As a matter of fact, during the time I was single and still trying to "make it" as an author, I spent every penny I made. I didn't care about saving. I was freshly divorced and could happily spend every dime on myself for the first time in over a decade, and no one could complain about it. So, I did.

I didn't worry about money *at all*. I didn't save for a rainy day or contribute as much to my 401(k) that I was "supposed" to. I just spent fearlessly. I figured I'd worry about the future later. At that time, I was focused on having fun, enjoying life, and chasing my dream of creating a new one.

After my two flopped books, I hired a publicist (who cost almost as much as my rent at the time) to help launch my next ones. I also bought an entirely new wardrobe, new hair, new makeup, a gym membership, and became a completely different person.

I had a blast becoming the new me, and then—*bam*. My third book took off in a completely unexpected fashion almost a week after it released.

I went from selling 101 books *total* for the month of January 2015 to 100 books *per hour* in February of 2015. Then my breakout book landed on *USA TODAY's* Best-Selling Books List three weeks in a row.

Along with knowing it would happen for me, believing it was coming, being totally fine with two flopped books, and generally living my best life at that point—spending fearlessly with faith and continuing to invest in my dream even when my publishing business was in the red could very well have been what pushed me over the line to the manifestation of my financial freedom.

I didn't really know any of the stuff in this book when it happened. I just believed in myself and the power of hard work.

But I remember, before that big demonstration of God in action, I was enjoying life and having fun chasing my dream and becoming the new me. I wasn't stressing about money—*at all*. I wasn't worried about the future or my retirement account. All I knew was that something great was going to happen for me.

And then it did, and it was a *big* something. A life-changing something.

Seemingly overnight, I had the financial freedom I had so desperately prayed for not even two years earlier. And I had a brand-new career doing something I loved.

Almost everyone I told my big dream to in the beginning probably thought I was at least partially nuts.

Watching it come true was *amazing*. Mind-boggling. Astounding.

I walked on clouds of gratitude and wonder. It was *awesome*. And I capitalized on all of it.

From my book sales, I saved the equivalent of two years' of income from my legal job in less than six months. And then, I quit.

Even with money in the bank, leaving my guaranteed job and

insurance behind still felt like jumping off a cliff. I prayed I'd learn how to fly before I hit the ground or ran out of money.

Instead, I soared.

Months after my dream came true, the Universe led me to Jake. Because that's what happens when you're working on yourself and chasing your dreams—the Universe pairs you with someone doing the same thing.

Like attracts like, remember? You attract who you are being. Be awesome and know it, and then . . . get your mind blown by how much God really loves you.

And Jake, well, he became what I lovingly call the "power ball" in my winning life's lottery.

Jake didn't realize it at the time, but he taught me how to dream even bigger. Reach even higher. Believe I was capable of even more. His influence gave me confidence in myself that I couldn't have acquired in any other way.

He taught me what it was to be truly fearless. He taught me what it meant to be myself, regardless if anyone liked me or approved of me. Jake opened a completely new infinite set of possibilities for me in life. Soul mates do that.

Never forget that there is more to life than money. *Ever.* Because if you do something only for the money, it's never going to lead you to lasting happiness, joy, or fulfillment. *Ever.* I know. I've done it twice and learned the lesson twice. It sucks.

Never forget that money is only a tool. It's super cool to have, and it makes life way easier. You are meant to have an abundance of it so you can have and do all things you want to do in this life.

But money will never buy you lasting happiness, no matter where you shop, how much you spend, or what you buy. I've tried that too. It's a hole in your heart that money and expensive purchases will never fill.

The best things in life truly are free. You don't need to be wealthy to have them. But there's no arguing that money provides greater freedom in today's world, and freedom is *always* a worthy goal. After all, that's why the Divine made you so powerful. So that you could be free to live this life as you choose.

**CHANGE YOUR THINKING.**
**CHANGE YOUR WORDS.**
**CHANGE YOUR BELIEFS.**
**CHANGE YOUR ATTITUDE.**
**CHANGE YOUR EMOTIONS.**
**CHANGE YOUR HABITS.**
**YOU WILL CHANGE YOUR LIFE.**

It's law.

They're all small things that only you control, and only you can change them.

They're free—but they're not cheap. You actually have to do it. And only *you* can do it.

**YOU ARE THE MAGIC INGREDIENT TO EVERYTHING YOU'VE EVER WANTED AND DREAMED ABOUT.**

*You.*

You are more capable than you've ever realized and powerful beyond your wildest dreams. You have everything it takes to start changing who you're being at any moment—and your entire world as a result.

You absolutely can do this. In fact, you incarnated in this body *to do this*. Whatever unconditionally loving and amazing future the Divine has planned for you is so perfectly wonderful, it would probably make you drop to your knees with joy and gratitude, thanking All That Is for Its astounding intelligence and generosity.

We know it's possible for you because it happened for us. We're not "special people." What happened for us wasn't a miracle. It was simply the workings of our consciousness and Universal Laws.

Anyone can change their life.

*Radically.*

And by doing so, help change the world for the better for everyone.

*Including you.*

Everything changes when you change.

And then magically, one day, you start waking up feeling like you've won the game of life....

# A FINAL WORD

There are levels to this game of life. That's something you learn as you grow in consciousness. We only know what we know right now, and we don't know what we don't know.

One thing is for certain: there's always more for everyone to learn, understand, and experience.

We wrote this book because we love you, even if we've never met you. We want the best for you. We want you to love yourself and your life. We know it's possible, because we live this way.

Our greatest hope is that something within these pages helps you along your journey. We offer it to you with love, from the great heart of the Universe itself. Take what resonates with you and leave the rest.

Thank you for your precious attention.

We hope you learned something positively life-changing.

*Love,*
*Meg & Jake*

# BONUS

If you want your life to be unrecognizable in the best way possible, here are ten things you can try:

1. Clean up your diet. Get rid of processed foods, sugar, GMOs, dairy, gluten, and anything not organic. Take a food-sensitivity test and a gut-health test to clean up the rest and commence an elimination diet.
2. Drink one gallon of water per day.
3. Move every day, at least fifteen to thirty minutes of activity to get your heart rate up.
4. Heal your gut. Stop taking over-the-counter meds like pain relievers, antacids, etc. Start taking high quality probiotics and gut-health-supporting supplements, if necessary.
5. Sit in silence for thirty minutes per day and learn to meditate.
6. Read positive, uplifting, and empowering books every day for at least fifteen minutes.
7. Practice gratitude, forgiveness, and surrender daily.
8. Quit watching TV, movies, and streaming services.

9. Quit scrolling through social media or quit it altogether if it's not part of your job.
10. Quit gossiping, complaining, worrying, stressing, judging, hating, and fearing anything and everything.

You don't have to make every change at the same time. In fact, there's a higher likelihood that you will to stick to these changes if you do them in stages.

Start with whatever calls to you and feels right or the easiest. Then keep adding good habits to your life one at a time. It won't take long before you're literally a different person and your life begins to change dramatically. It's law.

When you change your consciousness—who you are being—you change your life.

# WHO ARE WE?

**We live an unusual life.** That's why we wrote this book.

We don't live like "normal" people. We are the people most others would probably consider "weird." But because our life is *wonderful* and *amazing*, we thought we'd share some of our secrets because it turns out that being our kind of "weird" is also a codeword for being awesome.

So, who are we?

*We are creative rebels.* We know that we are each our greatest creative project in this lifetime. Our imagination is the most awesome power we've been given, and we use it to create our extraordinary lives and our extraordinary selves.

*We are totally health nuts.* We are. Absolutely. One hundred percent. Our entire life revolves around health and happiness. We are extremely choosy about what we put in, on, and around our bodies. We believe objects in motion stay in motion, so we move every day. Our bodies are our temples, so we take care of them with love.

*We work for ourselves.* We don't clock in or out. Our life includes our work and our work includes our life. We answer to no one except God.

*We are financially free.* We don't believe in debt. Freedom has always been our guiding light and will always be. We are sovereign beings.

*We educate ourselves.* We know education doesn't stop with traditional schooling, and we continuously learn new things. We understand that self-education is a unique source of power, and we double down on it because we love to learn, grow, and evolve.

*We are responsible for ourselves.* Our health, safety, and life are our own responsibility. We make our own decisions and live with the consequences of them. No one else is responsible for us.

*We dream big.* We know that it is just as easy to dream big as it is to dream small, and we choose to dream so big that it would scare normal human beings.

*We aspire to greatness.* We know that the concern is not in setting our goals too high and not meeting them, but in setting them too low and reaching them. We desire excellence in all things. We aspire to greatness because we are capable of it, and we believe we will achieve it.

*We dare greatly.* We know that the world is filled with people who will never dare anything at all, but we aren't those people. We came to shine brightly so that others know what is possible. In order to shine brightly, we dare greatly.

*We seek truth.* We know truth is love, and we seek it to improve our lives and the lives of others. We live for truth. We love truth.

*We don't care what other people think.* We know the most important thing is how we think about ourselves, so we don't waste time worrying about what other people think of us.

*We love our life.* We live an uncommon life because we are uncommon, and it is the most wonderful gift we've ever been given. We give thanks for our life and everything in it every day, all day long.

*We live from the heart.* We have lived for survival, achievement, and money. We have lived from a place of fear. Now we know there is no substitute for living from the heart. We feel our decisions in our hearts and our guts, and we listen to our intuition. It has never led us wrong.

*We grow and evolve.* We're not the same people we used to be. We are constantly becoming new and greater versions of ourselves. We will always be growing and evolving into the next better iteration of ourselves until we achieve mastery.

*We are unlimited.* We know the only true limits in life we face are those we impose upon ourselves. We choose to be unlimited.

*We choose love.* We choose love over fear and hate, every moment of every day. We forgive and we bless. We learn and we grow. We choose love because that is what we truly are.

We'd love to hear your positively life-changing stories.
Write to us at:
**love@creativerebel.com**

Want to hear from us? Become an official Creative Rebel by signing up for our newsletter here.

# ACKNOWLEDGMENTS

All Glory to God. This book is the direct result of prayer to be of service for the greatest good of humanity, and without the guidance of Infinite Intelligence and Unconditional Love, it would never have been written.

We stand upon the shoulders of giants. Special thanks to Florence Scovel Shinn, Ernest Holmes, Neville Goddard, Myrtle and Charles Fillmore, Dr. Joseph Murphy, John Randolph Price, Dr. David R. Hawkins, Esther and Jerry Hicks, Abraham, Don Miguel Ruiz, Emmett Fox, H. Emilie Cady, Dr. Bruce Lipton, Dr. Joe Dispenza, Dr. Tom O'Bryan, Dr. Joseph Pizzorno, Ann Boroch, Anthony William, Dr. Wayne Dyer, Eckhart Tolle, Michael Singer, Joel S. Goldsmith, Anita Moorjani, Norman Vincent Peale, Napoleon Hill, Paulo Coelho, Ben Angel, James Clear, Marianne Williamson, Gabrielle Bernstein, Christine Nazarenus, Dr. Anthony G. Jay, Manly P. Hall, Pedram Shojai, Andres Pira, Jackie Trepanier Simon, Chris Yonker, David Meltzer, Frank Zane, Alana Fairchild, Paramahansa Yoganada, Rumi, Guy and Edna Ballard, Michael the Archangel and the Angelic Host, Buddha, Krishna, Jesus Christ, Saint Germain and the entire Ascended Host, and many others whose influences, energies, teachings, and spiritual journeys have changed our consciousness irrevocably for the better. Thank you for your work, your words, your truth, and your love. We are eternally grateful for your efforts.

Massively special thanks, giant hugs, and unconditional love to both of our families. We would not be who we are without you. We are forever grateful for you.

In loving memory of Bob Cutler.

# NOTES

## Chapter 1

1. Paramahansa Yogananda, *The Second Coming of Christ: The Resurrection of the Christ Within You*, vol. 1 (Los Angeles: Self-Realization Fellowship, 2004), p. 8.
2. *The Count of Monte Cristo*, directed by Kevin Reynolds (Burbank, CA: Touchstone Pictures, Spyglass Entertainment, 2002).
3. *Webster's New International Dictionary*, 1st ed. (1932), s.v. "individual."

## Chapter 2

1. Joseph Murphy, *The Power of Your Subconscious Mind* (Englewood Cliffs, NJ: Prentice-Hall, Inc., 1963), p. 30.
2. Ibid., 31.
3. Ibid., 30.
4. Dr. David R. Hawkins, *Truth vs. Falsehood: How to Tell the Difference* (Carlsbad, CA: Hay House, Inc., 2005), xviii–xix.
5. Bruce H. Lipton, "Are You Programmed at Birth?: How to transform the subconscious trance," *Heal Your Life* (blog), Hay House, Inc., August 17, 2010, http://healyourlife.com/are-you-programmed-at-birth.
6. Lipton, "Are You Programmed at Birth?"
7. Bruce H. Lipton, *The Biology of Belief: Unleashing the Power of Consciousness, Matter & Miracles*, 10th Anniversary ed. (Carlsbad, CA: Hay House, Inc., 2005), 122.
8. Esther and Jerry Hicks, *The Law of Attraction: The Basics of the Teachings of Abraham* (Carlsbad, CA: Hay House, Inc., 2006), 33.
9. Ibid., 32–33.
10. Joe Dispenza, *Becoming Supernatural: How Common People are Doing the Uncommon* (Carlsbad, CA: Hay House, Inc., 2017), 33.
11. Ibid., 47.

## Chapter 3

1. Neville Goddard, *The Power of Awareness*. Pacific Publishing Studio, 2010. First published by G& J Publishing Company (Los Angeles: 1952), 5. Page

references are to the 2010 edition.
2. Ibid.
3. Ibid., 6.
4. Dispenza, *Becoming Supernatural*, 44.
5. Ibid., 46.
6. Hawkins, *Truth vs. Falsehood*, 282.
7. Dispenza, *Becoming Supernatural*, 44.

## Chapter 4

1. Florence Scovel Shinn, *Your Word is Your Wand*. Camarillo, CA: DeVorss Publications, 1978. First published 1928 by Florence Scovel Shinn (New York), 7. Page references are to the 1978 edition.
2. Ernest Holmes, *Creative Mind and Success*. New York: Dodd, Mead, & Company, 1957. First published in 1919 by McBride & Company (New York), 27. Page references are to the 1957 edition.
3. Florence Scovel Shinn, *The Game of Life and How to Play It*. New York: Florence Scovel Shinn, 1927. First published 1925 by Florence Scovel Shinn (New York), 7. Page references are to the 1927 edition.
4. Ibid.
5. Ibid., 7–8.
6. Miguel Angel Ruiz, M.D., *The Four Agreements* (San Rafael, CA: Amber-Allen Publishing, 1997), xiii.
7. Ibid., 25.
8. Ibid., 26.
9. Ibid., 27.
10. Ibid., 37.

## Chapter 5

1. Hawkins, *Truth vs. Falsehood*, 282.
2. Ibid., 404.
3. Ibid., 425.
4. Ibid., 426.

## Chapter 6

1. Norman Vincent Peale, *Enthusiasm Makes the Difference*, New York: Fireside, 2003, 27. First published in 1952 by Prentiss-Hall Inc. Page references are to the 2003 edition.
2. Ibid.
3. Shinn, *The Game of Life and How to Play It*, 1.

## Chapter 7

1. Manly P. Hall, *Magic: A Treatise on Natural Occultism*. Mansfield Centre, CT, 2014, 44–48. First published 1929 by Hall Publishing Company (Los Angeles). Page references are to the 2014 edition.
2. *Webster's New World Dictionary and Thesaurus*, 2nd ed. (2002), s.v. "constructive."
3. John Randolph Price, *The Superbeings* (New York: Fawcett Books, 1981), 26.

## Chapter 8

1. Matt. 18:3 (KJV).
2. Goddard, *The Power of Awareness*, 18.
3. Matt. 18:3 (KJV).

## Chapter 9

1. Andres Piro with Dr. Joe Vitale, *Homeless to Billionaire: The 18 Principles of Wealth Attraction and Creating Unlimited Opportunity* (Charleston: ForbesBooks, 2019), 99.
2. Tushar Vakil, "What Fears Are We Born With? Only Two!," Tushar Vakil (blog), November 27, 2018, http://www.tusharvakil.com/2018/11/27/what-fears-are-we-born-with-only-two-all-the-rest-of-them-are-acquired/.
3. Emmet Fox, *The Golden Key: Booklet #1* (Camarillo, CA: DeVorss & Company, 1931), 2.
4. Gabrielle Bernstein, *Super Attractor: Methods for Manifesting a Life Beyond Your Wildest Dreams* (Carlsbad, CA: Hay House, Inc., 2019), 66.
5. Bernstein, *Super Attractor*, 66.
6. Shinn, *The Game of Life and How to Play It*, 17-18.
7. Ibid.
8. Ibid.
9. Lipton, *The Biology of Belief*, 140.
10. Murphy, *The Power of Your Subconscious Mind*, 7.
11. *Ready Player One*, directed by Steven Spielberg (Burbank, CA: Warner Bros. Entertainment Inc., 2018).

## Chapter 10

1. *That Sugar Film*, directed by Damon Gameau (Los Angeles: Madman Production Company, 2015).

2. International Academy of Oral Medicine & Toxicology, "Fluoride Exposure and Human Health Risks: A Fact Sheet from the IAOMT," 2017.
3. Anthony G. Jay, Ph.D., *Estrogeneration: How Estrogenics Are Making You Fat, Sick, and Infertile* (Tallahassee, FL: Pyrimidine Publishing Company, 2017), 2-5.
4. Ibid., 4–5.
5. Dr. Tom O'Bryan, *You Can Fix Your Brain* (New York: Rodale Books, 2018), 72–73.
6. Ann Boroch, *The Candida Cure* (New York: Harper Wave, 2018), 74.
7. Ibid.
8. Ibid., 75.
9. Ibid., 83.
10. Joseph Pizzorno, *The Toxin Solution* (New York: Harper One, 2017), 75.
11. Ibid., 72.
12. Ibid.
13. Ibid.
14. Enjoli Francis, "Third US jury finds Roundup weed killer likely caused cancer, awarding couple $2 billion," ABC News, May 13, 2019, https://abcnews.go.com/Health/us-jury-finds-roundup-weed-killer-caused-cancer/story id=63015358.
15. Pizzorno, *The Toxin Solution*, 75.
16. O'Bryan, *You Can Fix Your Brain*, 68.
17. Boroch, *The Candida Cure*, 83.
18. "Big Food Companies Spend Millions to Defeat GMO Labeling," Environmental Working Group (blog), August 4, 2015, https://www.ewg.org/research/big-food-companies-spend-millions-defeat-gmo-labeling.
19. Grocery store flier from www.nongmoproject.org
20. Boroch, *The Candida Cure*, 77.
21. Christine Nazarenus, *Medical Cannabis Handbook for Healthcare Professionals*, New York: Springer Publishing Company, 2020), 29.
22. Ibid.
23. Ibid., 30.
24. Ibid., 31
25. Ibid., 30.
26. Ibid.
27. Boroch, *The Candida Cure*, 33.
28. O'Bryan, *You Can Fix Your Brain*, 57.
29. Ibid., 62
30. Ibid., 56.
31. Ibid., 57.
32. Ibid., 59.
33. Ibid., 329.
34. Ibid., 113.
35. C. Lee Ventola, MS, "*Direct-to-Consumer Pharmaceutical Advertising:*

*Therapeutic or Toxic?"* MediMedia USA, Inc., October 2011, https://www.ncbi.nlm.nih.gov/pmc/articles/PMC3278148/.
36. Rebecca Farley, *"Do Pharmaceutical Companies Spend More on Marketing Than Research and Development?"* Pharmacy Checker, July 24, 2020, https://www.pharmacychecker.com/askpc/pharma-marketing-research-development/#!.
37. O'Bryan, *You Can Fix Your Brain*, 58.
38. Ibid., 73.
39. Ibid.
40. *That Sugar Film*.
41. O'Bryan, *You Can Fix Your Brain*, 97.
42. Ibid., 97, 103.
43. Ibid., 100.
44. Pizzorno, *The Toxin Solution*, 47.
45. Pizzorno, *The Toxin Solution*, 217.
46. Anthony William, *Medical Medium* (Carlsbad, CA: Hay House, Inc., 2015), 265–266.
47. O'Bryan, *You Can Fix Your Brain*, 334.

# Chapter 11

1. Shinn, *The Game of Life and How to Play It*, 9.
2. Ibid., 10.
3. Ibid., 11.
4. Ibid., 12.
5. Ibid., 36.

www.ingramcontent.com/pod-product-compliance
Lightning Source LLC
Chambersburg PA
CBHW021442070526
44577CB00002B/256